Protecting Patients and Staff: Unarmed Response to Active Shooters in Healthcare

THE PLAYBOOK FOR SURVIVAL

Dave Young

Table of Contents

Disclaimer i

Dedicated ii

Acknowledgement iii

About the Author – Dave Young v

Foreword vii

Who is Vistelar? xvi

Chapter 1 Introduction to Safety and Preparedness in Healthcare 1

Chapter 2 What is an Active Assailant in Healthcare? 11

Chapter 3 Staying Calm and Safe in a Healthcare Setting 13

Chapter 4 The Importance of Healthcare Safety Protocols 19

Chapter 5 Managing Vehicle Emergencies in Healthcare Setting 22

Chapter 6 Recognizing and Reporting Warning Signs 27

Chapter 7 Response Strategies for Healthcare Settings 30

Chapter 8 Escape Barricade and Defend 44

Chapter 9 Escape Techniques and Assisting Others 61

Chapter 10 Top 10 Considerations for Barricading in Healthcare Settings 74

Chapter 11 Barricading Tactics in a Healthcare Environment. 79

Chapter 12 Defending yourself and others When You Can't Escape 88

Chapter 13 Providing Immediate, Self, and First Aid to Others 114

Chapter 14 Mental Health Support After an Incident 122

Chapter 15 Working with Hospital Security and Emergency Response Teams.. 131

Chapter 16 Conducting Exercises and Practicing Preparedness 136

Chapter 17 Reviewing and Updating Safety Protocols 143

Chapter 18 Supporting Each Other and Moving Forward After an Emergency 147

References... 158

Disclaimer

The information provided in this book is intended for educational purposes only. This is intended to be a part of and support the Training Program of Healthcare Workplace Violence Active Shooter Program, and collateral programs thereof.

The techniques and strategies discussed in this book are general guidelines to help individuals understand their options in an active assailant event. Every situation is unique, and actions should be taken based on the circumstances, individual judgment, and available resources at the time. Readers are encouraged to consult with local law enforcement, legal professionals, and emergency preparedness experts to tailor plans to their specific needs.

The author does not assume any responsibility for injuries, damages, or legal consequences resulting from using or misusing the information presented. Readers are solely responsible for their decisions and actions in any given scenario. Always prioritize safety, comply with local laws, and follow the instructions of emergency personnel.

Dedicated

As I dedicate this book, my heart swells with pride and aches for every healthcare professional who steps into the chaos of healing each day. This is more than a manual—it's a tribute to your courage, resilience, and sacrifice. Whether you wear scrubs, wield stethoscopes, push carts, or keep the hospital running in unseen ways, you are the backbone of patient care. You rush toward danger when others step away, armed not with weapons but with compassion, skill, and an unshakable sense of duty.

This dedication also carries a deeper weight—one that beats for my late daughter, Yashira Ortega. She was one of you, a warrior in healthcare whose light was stolen too soon. Her tireless dedication, her love for her patients, and her unwavering spirit fuel these pages. Writing this book is my way of honouring her memory and ensuring that those who stand where she once stood have the tools to protect themselves and their patients.

I write this with both grief and fire because I understand what's at stake. Lives hang in the balance, and you are the shield that stands between hope and tragedy. You do this not for recognition or reward but because it's who you are. So, I leave you with this:

Every tactic you practice is a deposit that extends your life or a withdrawal that shortens it. Train as if your next breath depends on it. And remember, your paycheck will never reflect the lives you impact, but the lives you save will forever carry your legacy.

Acknowledgement

Writing this book has been a journey made possible by the support, expertise, and encouragement of many exceptional individuals. I am profoundly thankful to the following people who have enriched this project with their diverse contributions:

Each professional named above brings decades of experience from the healthcare security industry, law enforcement, corrections, the U.S. military, and the private security sector, among other fields. Their extensive backgrounds have provided invaluable depth and perspective to this work, and I am honoured by their involvement.

With gratitude,

To the Vistelar team, whose dedication and insights shaped this work from the ground up:

- Gary Klugiewicz
- Thomas D. Poellot
- Tony Sherman
- Logan Lee
- Mike Delvaux
- Gary Drye
- Paul Carter
- Joel Lashley
- Ted Sandquist
- Special thanks to:

- Dale Hill, 3 decades of EMS and healthcare and emergency management experience.
- Marty Drapkin, 2 decades, Retired Wisconsin Department of Justice.
- Larry Hahn, 3 decades, Retired Law Enforcement, IOWA.
- Shawn Paul, over 3 decades of law enforcement and Healthcare Security.

About the Author – Dave Young

Dave Young is a highly respected expert in personal safety and defensive tactics, with extensive experience spanning civilian, law enforcement, healthcare, and the U.S. military sectors. Having survived his share of violent encounters from his youth into adulthood, Dave has dedicated his career to equipping others with the skills needed to stay safe in high-risk situations.

With over 35 years of combined experience as both a police officer and a veteran of the United States Marine Corps. Dave has built a reputation as a leader in security training. As a co-founder of Vistelar, he has trained professionals across the country and since 1990 has focused his expertise on enhancing safety in healthcare environments worldwide.

Dave's insights and expertise have been featured on CNN, Fox News, and the National Geographic Channel, solidifying his position as a trusted authority in the field. Dave is a weapons designer and author of "How to Defend Your Family and home sharing skills in surviving a home invasion.

This book is an essential resource for all healthcare professionals seeking to survive an active shooter attack. True safety lies in heightened awareness, the ability to recognize danger, and knowing how and when to respond. While no one can predict exactly how they will respond in a crisis, this is you "Playbook for Survival: provides real-world experience, critical knowledge and strategies to improve the chances of survival—both during and after such a traumatic event.

Foreword

Why did I write this book? I've spent over 35 years in high-pressure roles military, law enforcement, and tactical training—where I've seen firsthand how quickly situations can escalate. As a Co-Founder and VP of Training for Vistelar, my mission has always been to prepare people for the worst while equipping them with the tools to handle it effectively and compassionately.

The need for safety and preparedness in healthcare settings has never been more urgent. Healthcare professionals face unique challenges, navigating unpredictable emergencies while protecting patients, families, and themselves. From leading Special Reaction Teams to developing defensive tactics for professionals worldwide, my career has been dedicated to this very purpose. This book is the culmination of those decades of experience—designed to help you stay ready, stay safe, and respond with confidence.

The healthcare field is no stranger to emergencies, but the stakes are higher when lives depend on rapid and effective response. Whether it's managing an active assailant, addressing volatile patient behaviors, or responding to unforeseen crises like vehicle crashes into facilities, healthcare professionals need strategies that balance safety, empathy, and action. My mission is to equip you with knowledge and skills to remain calm, confident, and effective in the face of adversity. This is more than a guide—it's a call to action to safeguard the sanctity of healthcare spaces and the lives within them.

Healthcare staff often encounter situations that would make any reasonable person fear imminent harm or offensive contact. Many interactions involve individuals struggling with physical or mental health challenges—people who may not adhere to social norms, sometimes acting unpredictably in ways that can cause fear or even harm. These conditions, by their very nature, are the definition of assault, but in health care, they are often just considered part of patients' pathology. Or the stress of hospitalization. These same staff members are subject to that in the form of physical contact, ranging from mild to severe, which is defined as battery, but happens so frequently that it is considered part of the job. Many see it as part of the potential conditions and normalized environment in which care is provided. Customers of health care may not present their best selves forward, intentionally or otherwise. If the behavior of patients, family members, visitors, or even staff, is well outside of the social contract and causes the fear of, or actual, unwanted contact, this person is, by definition, an assailant. Staff, working in good faith, do not have the responsibility or even the time to attempt to understand the reasons why an assailant is engaging in a killing event or attempt to define it; they just need to survive. A singular, simple, well-rounded plan that will allow them to adjust to events gives them the best chance at survival when, if circumstances dictate, staff have to act.

The healthcare field is no stranger to emergencies of a varying and evolving nature, impacting not only healthcare workers but the vulnerable population in their care. The stakes are higher when life depends on rapid and effective response. Whether it's managing an active assailant, addressing volatile patient behaviors, or responding to unforeseen crises like vehicle crashes into facilities, healthcare professionals need strategies that balance safety, empathy, and action. My mission is to equip you with knowledge and skills to remain calm, confident, and effective in the face of adversity. This is more than a guide it's a call to action to safeguard the sanctity of healthcare spaces and the lives within them.

This book is a guide on how to identify, prevent, and respond to active *shooter* incidents, identify at-risk behavior, prepare for their occurrence, and, if such an incident occurs, have the best chance of survival for yourself and others. The number one goal is to survive an active shooter attack emotionally, mentally, and physically.

Active assailant incidents have arrived in our country and have rapidly become a common enough occurrence to present as a real threat to workers in the industry. If you conduct an online search for active assailant events, the return will be countless pages of results referencing dozens of incidents. An *active threat is a threat* defined as any incident that, by its deliberate nature, creates an immediate threat or presents imminent danger, regardless of the weapons or instruments used.[1]

Active shooters are offenders armed with a firearm who actively engage in killing or are attempting to kill people in a confined and populated area. If an offender is armed with another weapon (e.g., motor vehicle, knife, weapon of opportunity), they are called *active assailants* or *active killers*. Simply put, an active assailant event is a homicide in progress.

---

[1] (*Active Threat Preparedness | Safety | the George Washington University*, 2019)

While an active threat incident can occur spontaneously due to an emotional event in their life, many are preplanned.

This book is meant for anyone and everyone in healthcare who wants to learn more about active shooter preparedness. Please note, however, that local jurisdictions may vary by state statute, and organizational policies and procedures will dictate workplace responses. While the information in this book should have universal application, your local laws, policies, and procedures should always take precedence.

This book is just a fraction of the research and training we offer, and no one can predict every situation. However, it is intended to be used by healthcare professionals working in hospitals, clinics, and outpatient facilities who are dedicated to ensuring the safety of staff, patients, and visitors during potential active threat situations.

Active Assailant incidents in healthcare settings are critical events that have significant impacts on patients, staff, and the broader community. Understanding these incidents helps in developing better preparedness and response strategies. The following is a summary of five notable active assailant events in U.S. healthcare facilities, along with references for further reading. Healthcare has had its share of dangerous active assailant attacks.

In Portland, OR, at the Legacy Good Samaritan Medical Center Shooting on July 22, 2023, a security guard was shot and killed. The suspect was later killed by police in a nearby community. Initially, police responded to reports that a person with at least one firearm fired shots inside Legacy Good Samaritan Medical Center in Portland, the Portland Police Bureau said in a statement. Arriving officers searched for the assailant while working with hospital staff to treat the guard, who was transferred to another facility, where he later died. Police agencies from various agencies later tracked the suspect's vehicle to nearby Gresham, located about 15 miles (24 kilometers) east of Portland, where the vehicle was stopped. Officers shot and killed the suspect, and no police officers were injured, the release said. Since writing this book, and over a year after the incident, the victim's family is suing for 35 million dollars. [2]

In Tulsa, OK, at Saint Francis Hospital Shooting on June 1, 2022, a gunman entered the Natalie Building at Saint Francis Hospital in Tulsa, Oklahoma, killing four individuals, including two doctors, a receptionist, and a patient. The active shooter, who was a patient of one of the doctors, targeted his physician due to ongoing pain after back surgery. This tragic event underscores the potential risks associated with patient-provider relationships.[3]

In Chicago, IL, at Mercy Hospital Shooting on November 19, 2018, a gunman fatally shot his former fiancée, an emergency room physician, in the parking lot of Mercy Hospital in Chicago. The assailant then entered the hospital, killing a pharmacy resident and a police officer before being killed in a shootout with law enforcement. This incident highlights the dangers of domestic violence spilling over into the workplace.[4]

---

[2] (Vargas, 2024)
[3] (Deliso, 2022)
[4] (News, 2018)

On June 30, 2017, in New York City, at Bronx-Lebanon Hospital Center, a former employee of Bronx-Lebanon Hospital Center in New York City returned to the facility on June 30, 2017, armed with an assault rifle concealed under a lab coat. He opened fire, killing one doctor and injuring six others before taking his own life. The assailant had been terminated from his position two years prior, raising concerns about workplace violence and the need for effective employee off boarding procedures.[5]

On December 17, 2013, at Renown Regional Medical Center, in Nevada, a gunman opened fire at the Renown Regional Medical Center's urology office in Reno, Nevada, killing one doctor and injuring two others before committing suicide. In this case, the assailant was reportedly dissatisfied with the outcomes of previous treatments, emphasizing the importance of addressing patient grievances.[6]

The nature of workplace satisfaction and post-post-employment violence is still being defined.

As a father and now a grandfather, I often reflect on the answer I would give if I were ever faced with the heartbreaking task of going to a morgue to identify the body of a loved one who had fallen victim to such a tragic event. Until it is experienced, it is not real!

The question is: What was my loved one doing at the time of their death? I knew I'd likely get one of two responses, and I often wondered

---

[5] (Nir, 2017)
[6] (Hassan & Martinez, 2013)

which one I could live with for the rest of my life, even though both options were difficult.

The first response I could get is they were killed hiding behind somebody or under a bed or desk or inside a closet or bathroom. I know that an answer like that would enrage me, knowing that there are many things we can do in these tragic events to assist people to increase their survivability during these incidents.

Another answer I could get is that they were killed trying to escape while helping others get to safety or possibly disarming the assailant to save the lives of others. It was then and there that I decided I would want the second response for my own children. It is with that response in mind that I wrote this book.

On June 18, 1990, James Edward Pough entered the General Motors Acceptance Corporation (GMAC) office in Jacksonville, Florida, and opened fire, killing nine people and injuring four others before taking his own life. This attack, at that time, was considered one of the deadliest workplace shootings in U.S. history.[7]

It was a combination of all the active shooter incidents to that date and while I was on active duty in the United States Marine Corps that I started looking at these events occurring under a different lens.

What if a military member returned from deployment and found out that they were removed from the list to see his own kids? This is a person

---

[7] (*The Repossession of James Edward Pough: Mass Shooting, Baymeadows: Gilmore, Tim: 9781720528647: Amazon.com: Books*, 2025)

who trained in tactics. Would staying in the danger area save lives or increase the casualty rate?

I realized then what we were hearing from others to respond to active shooter situations was not accurate and there was a safer and more practical way to save lives. I started developing an unarmed and armed tactical response to active assailant attacks. Then, in July of 1999, after the Active assailant incident in Columbine in April of that year, [8]I started to research by reading, listening to others, attending classes, and watching videos. I realized the information that was being shared in the media or written in articles from newspapers or other spokespersons did not match the factual events that I have learned to be true through personal experience, professional training, and years of tactical incidents. I came to quickly realize that running was not specific enough and could create more confusion and chaos, hiding was extremely misleading and did not increase survivability, and without the right training when you hear the word fight - it was not direct and to the point enough to keep people safe. *This is discussed later in this book.*

However, what made tactical sense was the consideration of consequences during the decision-making process, so we developed 3 action words: titled ***Escape, Barricade, and Defend.*** With over 4 decades of experience and training in responding to these attacks as a law enforcement officer and United States Marine, I understood the goal is to save, preserve, and protect life.

---

[8] (FBI, 2019),

This is accomplished by immediately escaping from the immediate danger, that hiding just prolongs the inevitable. When escaping, you need to answer 3 important questions, including (1) how you get out of the danger area, (2) where do you go, and (3) what do you do when you get there will save your life If for any reason you are unable to **ESCAPE** regardless of the emotional, mental, and physical limitations you may have, the next immediate step is to **BARRICADE** yourself and others to preserve life. If you were unable to save yourself and others by **ESCAPING** or unable to preserve life by **BARRICADING** to give you more time to decide the best next course of action, then you would have to **DEFEND** yourself and others to protect life. This was the beginning of this journey to protect life.

Who is Vistelar?

Vistelar is a global training institute dedicated to training individuals and organizations on how to address conflict by building safe and respectful workplaces. Effective ways. By providing strategies for preventing problems before they arise and stopping threats when they occur, Vistelar aims to foster respectful and safe workplaces for all. Vistelar is a global training institute that helps individuals and organizations create safe, respectful workplaces by preventing conflicts and addressing threats effectively.

Training Programs

Vistelar offers a variety of training programs designed to promote safer and more respectful environments. Vistelar's training is organized into the following key areas:

1. Workplace Violence Prevention.
2. Non-Escalation, De-Escalation, and Crisis Management.
3. Personal Protection.
4. Positive Interventions.
5. Physical Alternatives.
6. Active Assailant Preparedness and Response.
7. Specialized Public Safety Training.
8. Instructor Development.

Over five decades of real-world experience support Vistelar's methodologies. These proven techniques are outlined in their acclaimed 'Confidence in Conflict' book series and are available through workshops, speaking engagements, and instructor schools. Vistelar uses online, virtual, and on-site methods to deliver training tailored to diverse needs.

Vistelar's Vision

The vision driving Vistelar is simple but profound: to make the world safer by encouraging people to treat one another with dignity and respect. This principle forms the foundation of every training program they offer.

Benefits of Training

Participants in Vistelar's training programs gain essential skills and knowledge to address active threat incidents effectively.

Understanding Active Threats

Active threat incidents, while rare, have become alarmingly familiar. A quick online search will yield countless results referencing tragic events. The list below highlights notable events; however, additional smaller-scale or less-publicized incidents may not be included. For the most comprehensive data, reviewing

Active Shooter Incidents at Hospitals (1990–2024)

1. Beaumont Hospital in Royal Oak, Michigan, on November 20, 1991, had 4 killed and 5 injured. (1991 Royal Oak Post Office

Shooting: The Untold Story of a Hero Who Gave His Life for Others, 2021)

2. Doctor's Hospital in Columbus, Georgia, on October 16, 2003, had 3 killed. [9]

3. Louisiana State Hospital in University in Shreveport, Louisiana, on July 22, 2005, had 1 killed. [10]

4. St. Vincent's Hospital in Birmingham. Alabama, on December 15, 2012, had 0 killed and 2 injured.[11]

5. Bringham and Women's Hospital, in Boston, Massachusetts, on January 20, 2015, had 2 killed (including the shooter). [12]

6. Bronx-Lebanon Hospital Center in Bronx, New York, on July 1, 2017, had 1 killed and 6 injured.[13]

7. Mercy Hospital and Medical Center in Chicago, Illinois, on November 19, 2018, had 4 killed (including the shooter).[14]

8. St. Francis Hospital in Tulsa, Oklahoma, on June 1, 2022, had 5 killed (including the shooter).[15]

---

[9] (WTVM, 2018)
[10] (KPLC, 2002)
[11] (*Gunman Shot Dead at St. Vincent's Hospital in Birmingham, Ala. - UPI.com*, 2025)
[12] (Payne et al., 2015)
[13] (Dienst, 2017)
[14] (News, 2018)
[15] (Hammond et al., 2022)

9. Sinai-Grace Hospital on May 3, 2023, in Detroit, Michigan, had 1 (the shooter died by suicide)[16]

10. Saint Luke's Medical Center on July 17, 2023, in Kansas City, Missouri, had 0 killed or injured.[17]

Although school-based events receive significant media attention, they account for only about a third of active threat incidents. The majority take place in 'soft target' environments, such as hospitals, clinics, workplaces, retail spaces, and houses of worship, where limited security measures often make them more vulnerable by design. This training focuses on strengthening these environments, transforming them into 'hard targets' to enhance safety and preparedness.

Unified Conflict Management System

The **6 C's of Conflict Management is** a representative model to show the nature of human contact. Designed to help individuals and organizations navigate challenging interactions, this approach emphasizes preparation, timely intervention, and the ability to de-escalate potential confrontations.

By focusing on key stages of conflict—Context, Contact, Closure, and the escalating phases of Conflict, Crisis, and Combat—this model guides responders through the entire process, from anticipating issues to fostering constructive outcomes. Whether managing day-to-day

[16] (Rock, 2024)
[17] (Dulle, 2024)

disagreements or high-stress encounters, the 6 C's provide a structured method to minimize harm and promote resolution.

This approach equips professionals with the tools needed to handle conflict with confidence, transforming potential disruptions into opportunities for better communication and stronger relationships.

The 6 C's framework provides a structured approach to analyzing and responding to conflict. It includes:

Vistelar's Unified Conflict Management System addresses every stage of human conflict, from prevention to resolution. This system incorporates:

1. The 6 C's of Conflict Management™ framework.
2. Consistent methods, principles, and terminology across programs.
3. Easy-to-apply techniques are illustrated through simple graphics and tools.
4. Universally applicable tactics emphasizing simplicity.

This comprehensive system ensures that the methods taught are easy to learn, apply, and remember. Core training programs include workplace violence, crisis management, and personal protection, supplemented with focused training on topics like chemical aerosols, and active assailant response.

1. Context: Preparation based on prior knowledge.
2. Contact: Managing the moment of interaction.

3. Closure: Ensuring positive outcomes and setting the stage for future interactions.

When conflicts escalate, they may progress to:

4. Conflict: Verbal misunderstandings or refusals.
5. Crisis: Situations exceeding a person's ability to cope.
6. Combat: Aggression or behaviors likely to cause harm.

The goal is to remain in the 'blue zone' of prevention and quickly de-escalate situations that enter the 'red zone' of conflict or crisis.

Workplace Violence Prevention

Workplace violence can take many forms, from verbal aggression to physical assault. Vistelar emphasizes prevention through:

1. Early identification of warning signs.

2. Establishing situational awareness.

3. Promoting a culture of respect and dignity.

Training empowers organizations to reduce risks and respond effectively to potential threats, creating safer and more resilient environments. Investing in resilience training enhances employees' problem-solving abilities, enabling them to navigate unique challenges with confidence. Additionally, resilience training programs have been shown to positively impact employees' mental health and well-being, further contributing to a safer organizational environment. [18]

Expanded Training Programs

The training programs offered by Vistelar are tailored to address a wide range of real-world challenges. For example, customer service training emphasizes techniques to handle difficult customers while maintaining professionalism. Conflict prevention programs focus on recognizing early warning signs of tension and implementing strategies to diffuse potential issues before they escalate. In physical violence management training, participants learn both verbal techniques and hands-on methods to control aggressive behavior safely.

In today's evolving conditions; these programs are indispensable for ensuring safety and fostering trust. Whether it's a workplace, healthcare setting, or public venue, Vistelar equips individuals with the skills necessary to navigate and resolve conflicts effectively.

[18] (Perelman, 2024)

A Vision for a Safer World

Vistelar is committed to making the world safer by promoting respect and dignity in all settings. The organization actively works to reduce conflict in everyday life by fostering respectful interactions. This approach has been shown to lead to improvements in community safety and cohesion. By focusing on environments such as schools and public spaces, Vistelar helps prevent conflicts and build stronger, more harmonious relationships.

Enhanced Benefits of Training

In addition to preparing individuals for active threat incidents, Vistelar's training programs provide lasting benefits, such as improved communication skills, greater self-confidence, and enhanced problem-solving abilities.

Participants in Vistelar's training programs have reported feeling more empowered to manage challenging situations in both their professional and personal lives. The training focuses on developing teamwork skills, helping participants collaborate effectively under pressure, which enhances their ability to handle conflict across various settings. These outcomes are supported by Vistelar's reputation in conflict management training, where skills learned are directly applied in real-world scenarios to improve communication, decision-making, and crisis response.

Participants often report feeling more empowered to address challenging situations both at work and in their personal lives. The training also promotes teamwork, as groups learn to collaborate effectively under pressure. These skills are not only valuable during crises but also contribute to overall personal and professional development. [19]

Addressing Active Threats in Diverse Settings

Active threat incidents can occur anywhere, from schools and hospitals to retail stores and places of worship. Each setting presents unique challenges. For example, hospitals must balance patient care with safety protocols, while retail environments must consider public accessibility. Vistelar's training addresses these diverse needs by tailoring strategies to fit specific environments. This adaptability ensures that participants are prepared to respond effectively, no matter the situation.

The Importance of the Unified Conflict Management System

The Unified Conflict Management System is a cornerstone of Vistelar's approach. By integrating the 6 C's framework with practical methods, the system offers a clear roadmap for managing conflict at every stage. Participants gain a deeper understanding of how to approach interactions thoughtfully, identify potential escalation points, and implement de-escalation techniques. This comprehensive approach ensures that conflicts are handled efficiently, minimizing risks for everyone involved.

[19] (Flipsnack, 2024)

Real-World Applications of Workplace Violence Prevention

Workplace violence prevention training is not just theoretical—it has practical applications in real-world scenarios. For instance, healthcare workers often face verbal abuse from patients or their families. With Vistelar's training, they learn to defuse anger and maintain a calm, professional demeanor, preventing situations from escalating into physical altercations. In retail environments, employees are taught to recognize suspicious behavior and respond proactively, ensuring the safety of both staff and customers.

Active Shooter Program Overview

Vistelar has developed an Active Assailant graphic that displays the systemized structure of methods of this training program.

In any active threat situation, it's crucial to maintain a clear focus on the top priority: Stop the Threat | Assist Victims. To achieve this, you must first Be Alert & Decisive and always respond, don't react. These principles should guide your actions both before and during the incident. Once an active threat is identified, your Survival Mindset must be activated immediately. This shift in thinking is essential for both personal and collective safety.

With these foundational principles in place, the next step is taking decisive action. The three key actions, **Escape, Barricade, and Defend**, are your best options for survival and ensuring the safety of those around you. Once the threat is neutralized, the situation should always conclude with Closure, ensuring that you and others can begin the process of recovery and healing.

Here is a brief orientation to this graphic:

Stop the Threat | Assist Victims is at the top to highlight these two primary goals of any active threat incident.

Be Alert & Decisive and Respond, Don't React are located on the sides to emphasize that these methods should be considered at all times before and during an incident.

Survival Mindset is next to indicate that this method should be applied immediately upon becoming aware of an active threat incident.

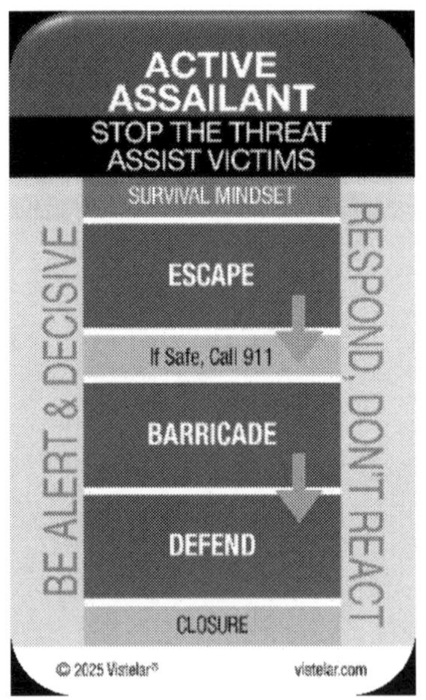

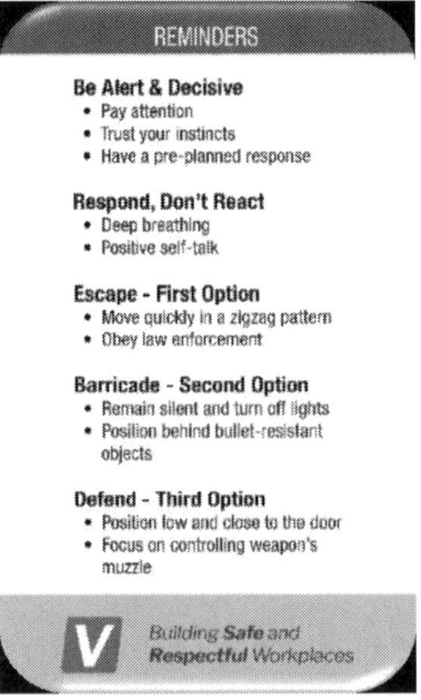

The center of the card lists the three appropriate actions that provide the best chance of your survival and the survival of others in the event of an active threat incident: **Escape, Barricade, and Defend.**

Closure is at the bottom of the graphic to indicate that this method should always be the final step of any active threat situation.

Active Threat Preparedness (Things you do before the attack)

An active threat is defined as any incident that by its deliberate nature creates an immediate threat or presents imminent danger.

An active assailant is an individual actively engaged in attempting to kill or cause serious bodily injury to others, typically in a confined and populated area. Unlike the term "active shooter," which specifically refers to individuals using firearms, "active assailant" encompasses attackers employing various weapons, such as knives or explosives.

There are three things your active threat preparedness plan needs to be successful:

Consider developing potential timelines for important processes. An initial timeline should outline clear and proactive hiring and termination procedures, established well in advance of any potential critical incident. This may include, but is not limited to, regular employee evaluations, performance management plans, and assessments to identify potential risks. For further guidance on creating effective hiring practices and monitoring for potential threats, please refer to the Workplace Violence Prevention and Intervention - Institution materials.

Additionally, identifying police timeline.

1. Ensure that everyone understands your various roles and responsibilities needed to be successful, and make sure those roles are within the abilities of assigned personnel.

2. Create a plan for sustainability through:
    a. Investing in training or instructors
    b. Reading articles
    c. Listening to podcasts and webinars
    d. Attending conferences on best practices
    e. Video reviews of incidents
    f. Daily Safety huddles
    g. Weekly briefings
    h. Monthly shift training
    i. Quarterly section drills
    j. Bi-annual organizational exercises

Before an effective active assailant response plan can be put in place, conduct a **Site assessment** of the current location, building structure, and staff schedules. This should include pictures of the area to describe the location in a residential or business area. Compare these pictures with the original diagram of the building, remembering that things change after construction.

It is important to identify the layout of the building to determine if it is a series of buildings that are clustered together or spread apart across a larger area. We also need to take into consideration the various levels of the building and whether it has an attic or a basement.

Make sure you take pictures from the front of the building to include the right, left, and rear of the building. This will help you identify if there are any obstacles impeding entry or exit points.

Confirm **Staff Readiness** to include conducting an organizational questionnaire and reviewing staff to assist in developing an effective active assailant response plan.

The first step is to evaluate the readiness of staff, including full- and part-time employees, volunteers, contractors, or other people who commonly enter and exit the buildings. Evaluating the readiness of all individuals who regularly access a facility—whether full-time or part-time employees, volunteers, or contractors—is critical in an active shooter response. In high-stress situations, people tend to react based on their level of training and preparedness. Ensuring that all personnel understand emergency protocols, know their roles, and can recognize potential threats before an incident occurs significantly improves response effectiveness. A well-prepared team can act decisively, follow established safety procedures, and help others, reducing chaos and increasing the likelihood of survival.

This includes understanding the training and experience individuals may bring from previous roles while also establishing and maintaining an annual in-service plan to support ongoing skill development.

My Nine Action Items I have identified:

1. **Action Item #1**: Developing and evaluating training programs to ensure staff are prepared to respond effectively in critical situations.

2. **Action Item #2:** Establish clear procedures for personnel entering the Human Resources (HR) department to ensure security and controlled access.

3. **Action Item #3:** Evaluate and address potential risks related to unauthorized individuals or intruders gaining physical access to the building.

4. **Action Item #4:** Assessing physical access to the facility through unconventional points, such as Windows, basements, vents, trash or laundry chutes and others. Potentially from older design schemes.

5. **Action Item #5:** Assess the visual deterrents that are in place

6. **Action Item #6:** Assess how unauthorized personnel can obtain access to sensitive semi secure areas of the building

7. **Action Item #7:** Identifying escape routes and places to assemble and the tools at hand to barricade these locations.

8. **Action Item #8:** First aid kits and materials to render aid First Aid kits are separate from patient care materials, and are specific to the threat they are built to treat. (GSW, Blast and Burn Kits) The staff are to be trained to use every item in each kit. The kits are to be inventoried regularly for completeness and expiration date of subcomponents.

9. **Action Item #9:** Sound Alert | Create Alarm

Below are the action steps needed to assist in asking the right questions and gathering information to create a plan. Take control of your safety; there is no such thing as an acceptable casualty. These are to be considered conceptual planning steps. At this current time, there is no known forecastable or identifiable data surrounding active shooter threats except for about a 50% current trend in shooters having behavioral concerns. Since active shooter events cannot be reasonably predicted, or prevented, we can focus on something we can impact, such as workplace violence events. The type of detailed background or security questioning required to screen for these threats are not anywhere the realm of allowable topics or questions towards employees. If an employee is identified as have behavioral concerns, labor laws press that accommodations are to be made to integrate them and make them feel comfortable. Your facilities HR may not allow targeting security investigation, and without probable cause, you very much be violating their civil rights. The behavior and mannerisms of individuals, especially those that fit the events' demographic, can be discretely observed by line supervisors and charge nurses who have immediate relationships with employees. Action Item #1: Preparing and assessing readiness training for staff:

1. Are employees required to attend and complete any formalize training related to managing conflict in the workplace?
2. Are employees required to attend and complete any form of training for de-escalation or crisis intervention in the workplace?

3. Are employees required to attend and complete any type of training for managing person(s) with special needs, learning disorders, or cognitive challenges?

4. Are employees required to attend and complete any type of training for the evaluation of procedures for fire emergencies and/or bomb threats?

5. Are employees required to attend and complete any type of training for preparing and responding to active assailant attacks?

6. Are employees required to conduct daily, weekly, end-of-shift, or any other form of ongoing refresher training for any of the above skills?

For an active assailant plan to be effective, the staff must maintain some level of understanding and readiness.

Action Item #2: Procedures for personnel entering Human Resources (HR) and reporting anything that may create an unsafe workspace:

1. What is the procedure for anyone entering the building/HR?

2. Who monitors this procedure for accuracy?

3. How often is this procedure checked?

4. What is the procedure or policy for staff notifications and reporting of suspicious activity?

5. What training does the HR staff receive for applying and reinforcing the staff notification policy for reporting suspicious behavior?

6. How often is this procedure checked?

7. When conducting exit or termination meetings, is it a policy to control the majority in the room? (Example – 1 female or male HR interviewing – HR has one female or male present in the room as well)

Once we assess the training and experience of the staff, we need to assess and understand the buildings and physical infrastructure we work in. This includes identifying exits and entrances and the fixed or roaming security posts. This also includes identifying which personnel have access to particular parts of the building, and who needs to be escorted throughout in access control areas.

Action Item #3: Assess access control protocols related to unauthorized access and an intruder's physical access to a building:

1. Is there a process for issuing keys, codes, and/or cards that require proper authorization, background checks, and the authorization of who has access to what?

2. Are access codes changed regularly to prevent unauthorized people from entering the area?

3. How many doors give access to this immediate area?

4. Which direction do these doors open/close? (This is important because if the door opens inwards, it fits into the safe place criteria) The safer place criteria mean you can see danger approaching, defend from this position, and escape if needed.

    a. Building structure

    b. Exterior to interior

    c. Entrances and exits

    d. Hallways and stairwells

    e. Open areas and offices

    f. Gathering places

    g. Classrooms and conference rooms

    h. Parking Structures

5. What is the construction material of those doors: wood, steel, glass supported, fireproof, etc.?

6. What types of hinges are used to hang the doors?

7. What type of locks are on the exterior building doors?

8. What type of locks are on the interior building doors that provide immediate access to the workplace?

9. Who is responsible for locking doors on access control and timers

10. Who is responsible for locking down key access doors?

In addition to access control and keeping lockable doors closed and locked, we also need to identify non-door entry points to the building. Windows, crawl spaces, and janitorial or maintenance rooms that are self-isolated need to be identified and assessed as well.

Action Item #4: Assessing physical access to the facility through windows:

1. Are the windows vulnerable to forced entry?
2. Do the windows have locks, and if so, what type? Who has access to the keys?
3. Are fences and/or walls in place, and do they adequately protect the property?
4. What condition are those barriers in?
5. Is the lighting sufficient to create a safe work environment and deter intruders?
6. How primary access to the facility is restricted (key, code, electronic card)?

One of the first lines of defense for an organization is to create visual deterrents. A visual deterrent is something that is seen before a person enters the property. These deterrents are in addition to steady reminders, such as signs that the facility's security measures are in place.

It could start with a small message on the company's website or include signs or posters that are visible to others as they enter or are on the property. Uniformed security staff are also a visual deterrent. Too often, workplaces post messages or posters in lobbies, bathrooms, hallways, breakrooms, lounges, or cafeterias instead of in the areas where they are most needed, such as restricted areas. Clearly visible video cameras, especially outdoor cameras starting at parking lots and staff entry areas, if this is different from the main entrance.

The presence of **gun-free zone** signs has been a topic of debate, with both advantages and disadvantages depending on perspective.

Advantages of Gun-Free Zone Signs:

1. Legal Clarity – Clearly designates areas where firearms are prohibited, helping law-abiding citizens avoid accidental violations of the law.

2. Creates a Perception of Safety – Some people feel safer knowing that weapons are not permitted in certain locations, such as schools, hospitals, and government buildings.

3. Liability Protection – Property owners and organizations can reduce liability by enforcing a strict no-firearms policy, potentially lowering legal risks in the event of an incident.

4. Supports Conflict De-Escalation – In sensitive areas like healthcare facilities, preventing firearms may reduce the likelihood of escalating violence.

Disadvantages of Gun-Free Zone Signs:

1. Potential Targeting by Criminals – Critics argue that gun-free zones can become soft targets, as attackers may assume there will be little to no armed resistance.

2. Limited Deterrence – Criminals intent on committing violence are unlikely to follow signage, meaning the law-abiding population is the only group affected.

3. Restricts Lawful Self-Defense – Concealed carry permit holders and off-duty law enforcement officers may be prohibited from carrying in gun-free zones, limiting immediate defensive responses.

4. Public Confusion and Enforcement Challenges – Without proper security enforcement, gun-free zone signs alone may not prevent someone from bringing a firearm into the area.

Whether gun-free zone signs provide more benefits than risks depends on enforcement measures, location-specific security strategies, and broader policies addressing active threats. Would you like additional references or studies on this topic?

Action Item #5: Assess the visual deterrents that are in place:

1. What signs are in place alerting others that they are entering a restricted or monitored area?

2. Are the signs clearly posted and appropriately placed?

3. Are security personnel used at or near these areas?

4. Are security personnel uniformed or non-uniformed/in plain clothes?

5. Are security personnel armed or unarmed?

6. If security personnel are used, what is the level of training for their position?

7. Are there pull-down alarms in or close to the work area?

8. Are there evacuation plans posted at exits and entrances and near every office?

9. Are evacuation drills conducted?

10. Do detection and monitoring devices alert the appropriate personnel?

11. How often are inspections done? By whom?

12. Are there fire extinguishers in the room?

13. How often are evacuation drills conducted and chaptered, and by whom?

14. Who is responsible for checking exterior lighting?

15. Clearly vision video cameras, whether they are functional or they are blank decoy cameras, can be placed in areas of egress and exit. It gives the perception that it is hard to scout or plan for an event discretely. Concern of being seen is a great deterrent.

The ability to control movement within your buildings is another way to increase site safety. It is important to identify the typical pedestrian flow, including where they enter the building, through what door, where they conduct their business, and where they exit the building and property.

Action Item #6: Assess how unauthorized personnel can obtain access to restrictive areas of the building:

1. What is your Visitor Management process to identify visitors, who they are visiting, and where they should be located within the building?
2. Are security personnel always in place to watch the cameras?
3. How quickly are badges or IDs issued, changed, and discontinued?
4. Are background checks performed?
5. Do all employees wear photo ID badges?
6. Do visitors wear badges, and are they different from regular employees?
7. Are maintenance staff or contractors escorted or monitored closely?
8. Are there security cameras on the property? Cameras are a great deterrent; even blank cameras can discourage planning and trespassing if they give the appearance of good coverage and visibility. A good spread of manned cameras and blanks can be both a deterrent and allow detection and monitoring.

a. How many?

b. Where are they positioned?

c. Are they monitored?

d. How often is the footage reviewed?

e. Have blind spots been identified?

f. How many frames per second do they record?

g. How far do these tapes go back, or are they looped and copied over after a specific time?

h. Are these tapes logged and stored on clouds or storage drives?

i. Identify processes for reviewing video footage, storing the footage, and releasing it to law enforcement (court-ordered and exigent circumstances).

All these questions are important because many times when a person is terminated all of their access to the building (including ID and access badges) is surrendered back to the organization. This will limit their ability to enter the property at will or under the radar.

There are many stories of employee termination where they have used their own (or unaccounted for) access badges to enter the building. This usually results in a verbal or physical altercation or, in some cases, an active assailant attack.

There have been instances where former employees used their access credentials to re-enter workplaces and commit attacks:

1. **2019 Virginia Beach Shooting**: DeWayne Craddock, a former public utilities engineer, resigned from his position but retained his security pass. He used this access to enter the municipal building and fatally shot 12 people. (Wikipedia Contributors, 2025)

2. **Washington Navy Yard Shooting (2013)**: Aaron Alexis, a former Navy contractor, used his valid contractor ID badge to gain access to the Navy Yard. He then carried out a shooting that resulted in 12 fatalities.[20]

These incidents highlight the critical importance of promptly revoking access credentials of departing employees to enhance workplace security.

Action Item #7: Identifying escape routes and places to assemble:

1. Have escape routes been identified for each workspace?
2. Have escape drills been conducted to ensure they are within the emotional and physical limitations of your patients and staff?
3. Have assembly areas been identified for the accountability of staff?
4. Have the staff been assigned teams for designated areas?

[20] (Washington Navy Yard Shooting, 2022)

5. Do all staff know the best rooms to barricade and the ones to avoid that do not offer escape options?

In our program, the first thing we emphasize is to escape danger. This means you must identify an escape route before entering the building or office. This can be difficult for some, as some locations may not offer a safe escape route, meaning you will either have to get out of the building immediately or go to another room.

The first thing we need to do is identify the safest way to exit the building or space we are in. This could be through an adjacent door, a window, a crawlspace, or a vent. If no place exists, immediately get out of that room and go to another location. If you are unable to exit the space, immediately barricade that room and be prepared to defend it if necessary.

We have developed criteria for identifying a safer place to go, which is a location where:

1. You can quickly and easily exit
2. You can see danger coming
3. You can defend yourself from

If you are unable to do all three things, then you did not pick an optimal place for safety.

Pre-determine optimal and possible assembly areas. These assembly areas, or areas of refuge, should not include the same locations identified in your fire evacuation plan, as they are generally in the direct line of sight of the building and, therefore, create the potential for people to remain accessible to the assailant.

Consider locations that:

1. Are accessible to all people with varying emotional and physical capabilities.

2. Are likely to provide cover, barriers, or at the very minimum concealment from the assailant "cover" is something, such as a concrete wall or pillar, that can stop bullets, whereas "concealment" is something that merely hides or conceals you from view, such as a flipped-over folding table).

3. Are accessible to first responders and large apparatuses, such as armored vehicles or ambulances.

4. Have cell service and the ability to make external communication.

Additionally, keep in mind that active threats can be disgruntled employees, often former employees who are familiar with organizational evacuation plans and may be aware of your assembly locations.

Action Item #8: First aid kits and materials to render aid:

1. Are there first aid kits on the property, and if so, are they immediately accessible throughout the building/property rather than being positioned in a central location?

2. Are employees required to attend and complete any training for administering immediate aid to self and others?

3. Are employees required to attend and complete any type of training for rendering self-aid in emergencies, such as treatment for shock, serious injury, or a gunshot wound? First aid kits are most effective when small, light, transportable, and built directly for a specific threat, such as a burn kit, a GSW kit, and a blast kit.

4. How often and to what extent is your first aid training conducted through accredited organizations?

5. How is it chaptered, and how is proficiency measured?

When thinking about administering first aid and what materials are needed to render aid, break them into three separate categories.

1. Immediate aid. This is for when you need to immediately stop the bleeding in the case of a gunshot wound and the need to get to a safe place to render aid to yourself. Immediate aid could include applying direct pressure and inserting a finger into the wound to stop the bleeding, allowing you to get up and move to a safer location to render self-aid.

2. Self-aid. This is when you will use actual medical equipment to provide self-aid. This could be the sole application of a tourniquet, compression bandage, or splint without anyone else around to help you. Being able to perform self-aid is extremely important and should be the number one type of first aid training received, as you may need to administer self-aid until advanced medical professionals arrive.

3. First aid. This is when medical equipment and supplies are administered to you by trained emergency medical staff when they arrive. This is why immediate aid and self-aid are extremely important and should be covered in your training plan.

Action Item #9: Sound Alert | Create Alarm:

1. Is there a building-wide code to activate your active assailant plan?
2. Is this building-wide code tested quarterly, bi-annually, etc.?
3. Is there an emergency operation plan for mass communications for initiating your active threat response plan?
4. Is this agency-wide code tested quarterly, bi-annually, etc.?
5. Is there a building-wide public address code in place to initiate your active assailant plan?
6. What procedure is in place to notify the police of an active assailant in your workplace?
7. Is this procedure tested quarterly, bi-annually, etc.?

When you become aware of an active assailant, it is necessary to Sound Alert | Create Alarm. Part of sounding alert is the ability to project your voice (yell out to others) to warn them of the emergency. It also includes calling the police and knowing exactly what to say.

A few examples of this are:

1. Sounding Alert in the immediate area could include a nonverbal cue of raising both hands above your head, jumping up and down, demonstrating a stop sign, or pointing down the hallway to signal that an active assailant is in the building, and you need to start your active assailant plan.

2. Ensure you speak loudly so that everyone can hear you and tell them to exit the area.

Create Alarm consists of using the right word choice to inspire action to be taken by others; in this case, to activate the active assailant plan. When calling and notifying the police, you must follow a specific procedure to ensure the best response.

BEFORE MAKING THE 911 CALL, MAKE SURE YOU ARE IN A SAFE LOCATION.

That means being in a location where you cannot be seen or heard by others, especially the assailant(s).

Begin autogenic breathing to stay calm, then call 911 for help.

Autogenic breathing is a controlled breathing technique used to reduce stress and promote relaxation. It involves taking slow, deep breaths, focusing on exhaling longer than inhaling, which helps calm the body and mind.

Answer the questions the emergency operator asks you and only answer those questions. Try to leave your emotions out of it as it will slow down and delay getting help to your location.

For example:

1. The operator says, "Is this an emergency?"
2. Respond with "Yes."
3. The operator may say: "State the emergency" or "What is the emergency?"
4. Respond with: "My name is ______, and I'm located at 123 North Adams Street at the Angels Hospital, and we have an active assailant in the building." Then stop talking.
5. The operator may pause before asking additional questions, as they are likely already mobilizing and coordinating officers to respond to the scene.
6. Answer all the follow-up questions as clearly and concisely as possible. They will likely ask you for the last known location of the assailant(s) and any definitive description of the assailant(s) you can provide.

A word of caution: people calling in these incidents often report that they believe there are multiple assailants when that is rarely the case. This is partially due to the acoustics in the building (making it difficult to determine where the shots are coming from) and also by relaying conflicting subject descriptions (an assailant could easily be misidentified by gender or race, the clothing colors may be perceived differently by different people, and people have varying ability to accurately describe weapons). One tactic you can use if you are in an area and hear what appears to be gunshots is to immediately take cover and watch the movement of others around you. In many places, without taking cover, you may be running away from the echo, which, in reality, brings you directly into the assailant's location. If possible, watch the ground for bullets that might ricochet, which may be an indicator of the direction of the assailant.

There are a few questions to answer before reporting these attacks, and word choice makes all the difference when describing the assailant to the dispatch center. It is best to report first-hand information and not what someone else told you.

1. Did you see the person(s)?
2. Were they holding a firearm?
3. Can you describe it?
4. Did you see them shoot someone?
5. What part of the facility were they shot and where?
6. How many people did you see get shot?

Putting It All Together

After you complete the organizational questionnaire, review the pictures and videos and write down any additional comments, questions, or concerns that came up as you went through the process.

Record the date and time the assessment was completed and state your position and role within the organization. Add the names of any additional staff who assisted.

Review the assessment and conduct it yearly as building layouts and personnel change. It is critically important to maintain current information so you and your organization can make the best decisions in emergencies and increase survivability.

Organizational active threat preparedness also includes adopting and following workplace violence prevention policies and procedures, which may include:

1. Adopting Vistelar's Treat People with Dignity by Showing Them Respect philosophy.

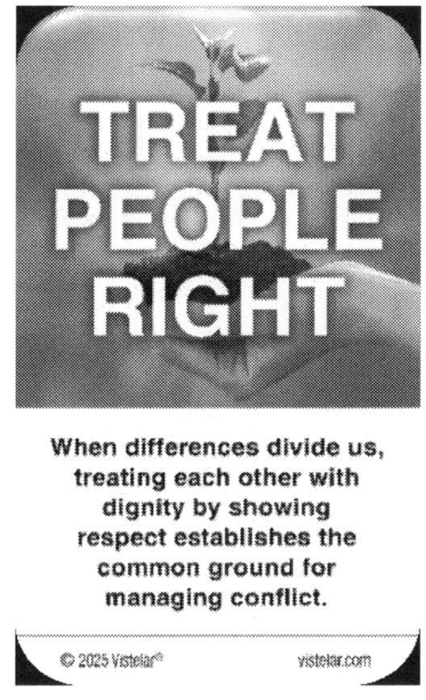

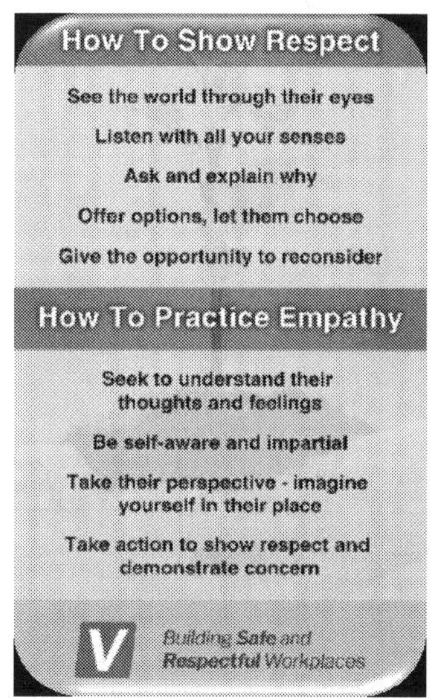

2. Establishing a Social Contract on how everyone is treated throughout the organization

3. Forbidding Gateway Behaviors (cursing and shouting at employees, intimidation, hazing, and disrespectful behavior towards others) and if they occur, responding appropriately

4. Mandatory reporting of pre-incident indicators, overt threats, and workplace violence incidents, with impunity and anonymity if desired

    a. The phrase "See something, say something" was first popularized by the New York Metropolitan Transportation Authority (MTA) in 2002. It was created as part of a public safety campaign designed by the advertising agency Korey Kay & Partners in the aftermath of the September 11, 2001, terrorist attacks. [21]

    b. The slogan encourages citizens to report suspicious activity to authorities, emphasizing the role of public vigilance in preventing potential threats. Over time, the phrase has been widely adopted across the United States and internationally as a cornerstone of counterterrorism and community safety campaigns.

5. Frequent mandatory training in How to Treat People with Dignity by Showing Them Respect, threat assessment, and safety measures

Assessing the Importance of Conducting Workplace Safety

[21] (Wikipedia Contributors, 2025)

A workplace safety assessment is a systematic evaluation of potential risks and vulnerabilities within an organization. This initial hazard assessment serves as a foundation for improving preparedness, particularly for active assailant incidents.

The Workplace Safety Assessment tool provides a structured approach to measuring an organization's Safety Rating, offering insights into strengths and areas for improvement. The rating is determined by assigning:

- Two points for each "yes" response
- One point for each "no" response
- Total score calculation to determine preparedness levels:
    - Trained & Prepared (50-40 points)
    - Untrained & Unprepared (39 points or below)

The assessment evaluates key security measures, including physical deterrents, access controls, monitoring practices, staff observation, and active assailant training. By implementing this process, organizations can systematically enhance their safety protocols, staff awareness, and emergency response capabilities to create a more secure environment.

Location	Yes/2	No/1	Comments
Open area to build and property			
Closed area to building and property (sealed off from the public)			
Gated/Chained areas			
Visual Deterrents			
Police On Property – (Uniformed) Armed or Unarmed			
All entrances are secured to gain access from outside.			
The property is video recorded only.			
The property is video recorded and monitored daily.			
Property I video recorded and reviewed (Weekly, Monthly, Quarterly)			
Physical Deterrents			
Posted Security Guards Unarmed or Armed			
Police or Police Vehicles on the property			
Key Access Only areas			
Monitoring			
Physical walk-through of common areas and grounds (before, during, and after hours)			
Staff outside of the hospital between shifts			
Additional persons who volunteer their time			
Designated staff walking through hallways and common areas			
Administration being more interactive with staff.			
Staff Observation and Challenges			

Staff visually check IDs, Uniforms of others.			
Staff verbally challenge other staff.			
Staff verbally challenge volunteers			
Staff verbally challenge contractors.			
Training			
All staff have been trained in their roles and responsibilities for Active Assailant			
All Supervisors trained in their roles and responsibilities for Active Assailant.			
All work sections conduct weekly or monthly training.			
All work sections conduct quarterly scheduled or unscheduled exercises.			
Hospitals conduct bi-yearly scheduled or unscheduled exercises with local law enforcement, and community groups for Active Assailant Response			
Additional Comments on the back			**Total**

Organizational Safety Survey

Conducted by:________________ ____________________

Additionally, if you observe any violations of workplace violence prevention policies and procedures, document and report them. Effective enforcement is essential to maintaining a safe work environment, as policies and procedures hold little value if not upheld.

If you are asked to gather data on your organization's policies and procedures, contribute to these efforts to help ensure they align with best practices.

Identifying Threats and Increasing Awareness

Threat assessment is the practice of determining the credibility and seriousness of a potential threat (whether something is an actual, or potential threat) as well as the probability that the threat will become a reality (determining the intent and capability of the threat factor).

On the most basic level, threat assessment aims to interrupt people on a pathway to violent behavior.

Threat assessment, in a given situation or of a specific person, is a continuous process. It is not something you do "just one time." Another issue that contributes to a harmful and aggressive workplace culture is a lack of basic assessment skills.

It is not something you do "just one time." Another issue that contributes to a harmful and aggressive workplace culture is a lack of basic assessment skills. We are generally poor at recognizing the cycle of violence and, as a result, we don't share known information about a particular person or event.

The better we are at identifying pre-incident indicators or precipitating events (red flags), the better we will be at preventing or avoiding potentially dangerous situations. These red flags are often identified after the fact, causing us to say things like, "Oh, wow, I should have seen that coming—all of the signs were there!" The goal is to identify these behaviors on a timeline—before the "impact" of the event.

Violence does not just happen out of the blue. The path toward violence is an evolutionary one with signposts along the way. This is known as "leakage." When we review the entire sequence of events leading up to the last acts, we readily recognize a series of behaviors and events that led down the path and set the stage for violence. Those details offered clues into what was coming in the form of conflict, broken relationships, antisocial behaviors, implied threats, social media postings, and explicit threats. This dispels the myth that "they just snapped." Reminding yourself that some of these behaviors may not be present at all.

If someone had done something differently at a specific point in the timeline, the violent outcome may never have come to pass. Hindsight is 20/20 because it is easy to recognize the first acts of violence when we know how they end.

It's important to note that these symptoms are not exclusive to any single diagnosis and require comprehensive evaluation by mental health professionals. Here are some disorders and conditions that could cause these behaviors:

1. Intermittent Explosive Disorder (IED):
    a. Characterized by sudden episodes of unwarranted anger, verbal outbursts, and physical aggression.
    b. Symptoms: Outbursts of anger, increasing belligerence, and failure to take responsibility for actions.
2. Oppositional Defiant Disorder (ODD) (typically diagnosed in children and adolescents)
    a. Marked by a pattern of angry, argumentative, and defiant behavior.

b. Symptoms: Angry/argumentative behavior, blaming others, and hypersensitivity to criticism.

3. Antisocial Personality Disorder (ASPD)

    a. Involves a pervasive pattern of disregard for the rights of others, deceitfulness, and lack of remorse.

    b. Symptoms: Retaliation against perceived injustice, failure to take responsibility, and preoccupation with violent themes.

4. Borderline Personality Disorder (BPD)

    a. Includes intense and unstable interpersonal relationships, impulsivity, and emotional dysregulation.

    b. Symptoms: Outbursts of anger, noticeable changes in behavior, and hypersensitivity to criticism.

5. Post-Traumatic Stress Disorder (PTSD)

    a. This is caused by exposure to traumatic events, leading to hypervigilance, irritability, and difficulty managing anger.

    b. Symptoms: Preoccupation with violent themes, hypersensitivity to criticism, and outbursts of anger.

6. Major Depressive Disorder (MDD) with Psychotic Features

    a. Severe depression may include irritability, suicidal/homicidal thoughts, and psychosis.

b. Symptoms: Homicidal/suicidal comments or threats and noticeable changes in behavior.

While not always predictive of violent behavior, specific, identifiable behaviors of concern include:

1. Often exhibiting angry or argumentative behavior
2. Consistently blaming others for their problems
3. Failing to take responsibility for their actions
4. Retaliating against perceived injustice
5. Increasing belligerence
6. Ominous, specific threats
7. Hypersensitivity to criticism
8. Recent acquisition/fascination with weapons
9. Preoccupation with violent themes
10. Interest in recently publicized violent events
11. Outbursts of anger
12. Extreme disorganization
13. Noticeable changes in behavior
14. Homicidal/suicidal comments or threats

No single behavior predicts that someone will engage in an active assailant event, but a combination of several behaviors may indicate a potential threat. Recognizing these warning signs and understanding their significance is crucial in preventing such incidents.

Chapter 1

Introduction to Safety and Preparedness in Healthcare

Safety in healthcare facilities is crucial, not only for the well-being of patients but also for staff and visitors. In a healthcare setting, violence can arise at any moment, and preparing for it can make all the difference. This chapter introduces the importance of safety and preparedness, especially in situations involving active assailants. When healthcare staff are prepared, they know how to stay calm, think clearly, and take appropriate action to keep everyone safe.

Preparedness means understanding the potential risks, being aware of the surroundings, and knowing the steps to take in an emergency. The Active Assailant guidelines emphasize that being unprepared increases the risk to everyone. By paying attention to early warning signs, staying aware of their surroundings, and having a proactive response plan, healthcare teams can create a safer environment for everyone. In this chapter, we will discuss the unique aspects of preparedness within healthcare and the steps each person can take to contribute to a safe and secure environment.

Why are Safety and Preparedness Important in Healthcare?

Healthcare facilities are busy places where patients, staff, and visitors come and go every day. Unlike other public places, healthcare settings are filled with people who may be vulnerable due to illness or injury. This makes safety even more important.

When staff are prepared for emergencies, they can respond quickly and confidently. Being prepared can prevent harm, reduce panic, and ensure everyone knows what to do if something goes wrong. In a healthcare environment, where every second counts, a well-prepared team can make a big difference in keeping everyone safe.

Understanding Different Types of Emergencies

Emergencies ranging from medical to violence in healthcare facilities can include natural disasters like earthquakes or floods, fires, and violent incidents such as active shooter situations. Each type of emergency requires different actions, but all of them need quick thinking and a calm response.

Active assailant situations are especially challenging because they can happen without warning and put many people in danger. In these situations, knowing the facility layout, having clear communication channels, and understanding how to protect oneself and others are essential. Healthcare facilities should have plans in place for all types of emergencies, and staff should be familiar with these plans.

The **First Responder's Philosophy (FRP)** provides a clear and structured approach to managing emergency situations. It consists of **ten steps** designed to ensure a systematic response, starting with **awareness** and progressing through to **debriefing**. The first step, **Arrive**, is about recognizing the emergency and establishing situational awareness. This sets the stage for the remaining actions that follow.

Once the situation is identified, responders **assess** the nature of the emergency—whether it's a disturbance, medical emergency, fire, or other incidents. This assessment helps guide further action. The next step, **Alarm**, involves notifying internal and external personnel and ensuring that the right resources are on the way. Once help is called, it's time to **evaluate** the situation, considering the threats and risks involved, as well as any hidden dangers that might pose a challenge. If the environment is deemed safe, responders can **enter** and begin their intervention.

After entering the scene, it's crucial to **stabilize** the situation using verbal or physical techniques. At this point, the responders check the **medical status** of any individual involved, assessing vital signs like breathing, airway, and circulation (often referred to as BAC). Treatment should be applied based on the responder's training, and if necessary, **EMS** (Emergency Medical Services) should be activated. Responders should stay close to the affected individuals, continuing to monitor their condition long-term.

In addition to providing medical care, **communication** is key. Throughout the process, responders should relay **who**, **what**, **where**, **when**, and **why** to ensure that everyone involved is on the same page.

Once the situation is under control, it's essential to **document** the incident and conduct a **debriefing**. This allows for a comprehensive report of the event and provides an opportunity for lessons learned, ultimately improving future responses to similar emergencies.

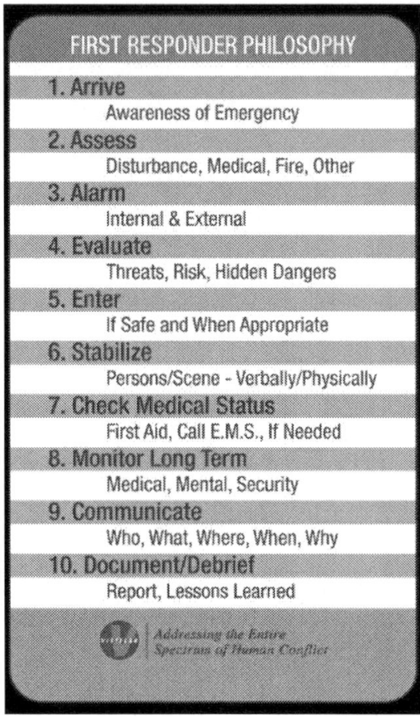

Summary of the First Responder's Philosophy (FRP) 10-Step Process

The **First Responder's Philosophy (FRP)** outlines a structured **10-step approach** for effectively managing emergencies, ensuring safety, and minimizing risks.

1. **Arrive** – Recognize the emergency and maintain situational awareness.

2. **Assess** – Identify the nature of the incident (disturbance, medical emergency, fire, etc.).
3. **Alarm** – Notify appropriate personnel and emergency services.
4. **Evaluate** – Assess potential threats, risks, and hidden dangers.
5. **Enter** – Proceed only if the scene is safe and conditions are appropriate.
6. **Stabilize** – Control the situation using verbal or physical techniques.
7. **Check Medical Status** – Evaluate breathing, airway, and circulation (BACs), assess injuries, provide necessary treatment, and activate EMS if needed.
8. **Monitor Long-Term** – Observe medical, mental, and security concerns to ensure continued safety.
9. **Communicate** – Clearly relay key details (who, what, where, when, why) to necessary personnel.
10. **Document/Debrief** – Complete reports and conduct a review to improve future response strategies.

This step-by-step process ensures **a coordinated, efficient, and effective response** to emergencies, prioritizing **safety, communication, and proper medical intervention**.

The Role of Situational Awareness

Situational awareness means paying attention to what is happening around you. In a healthcare setting, this means being alert to anything that seems out of place or unusual. Staff members should be aware of who is entering and leaving the building, watch for any strange behavior, and stay informed about what is happening in their area.

Being aware of early warning signs, like someone acting suspiciously or hearing unusual sounds, can help staff respond quickly. Practicing situational awareness helps everyone stay prepared and reduces the chance of being caught off guard in an emergency.

Early Indicators of Threats

Active assailant situations may sometimes have warning signs before they happen. These signs could include someone expressing anger, acting aggressively, or showing unusual behavior. Other indicators might be physical, such as someone carrying a large bag or moving in areas they aren't supposed to be. Gathering close to entrances and exits without purpose.

Recognizing these early indicators can be an important step in preventing escalation. If staff members notice anything unusual, they should report it to security or a supervisor. By staying alert to these signs, healthcare staff can play an active role in keeping the facility safe.

Having a Proactive Response Mindset

A proactive response mindset means being ready to act before an emergency gets worse. It involves taking steps to prepare in advance and knowing how to react if something happens. In a healthcare setting, this includes practicing emergency procedures, staying calm, and helping others stay calm, too.

When everyone has a proactive response mindset, it creates a safer environment for everyone. Staff can practice this mindset by participating in drills, reviewing safety procedures, and talking with team members about what they would do in different situations. Being prepared and ready to respond can save lives and reduce harm.

Creating a Culture of Preparedness

Preparedness is everyone's responsibility, and it starts with building a culture of safety. This means that everyone, from volunteers to the CEO, understands the importance of safety and knows their role in an emergency.

Healthcare facilities can support this culture by providing regular training and drills, encouraging open communication about safety, and reminding everyone to stay aware of their surroundings. When everyone feels responsible for preparation, the whole team works together to create a safer environment.

Active Assailant Preparedness Guidelines

The Active Assailant Preparedness guidelines are a set of recommendations designed to help healthcare facilities prepare for potential violent incidents. These guidelines emphasize the importance of being aware of surroundings, watching for warning signs, and knowing how to respond.

Your guidelines need to suggest that staff should stay calm, think clearly, and follow established safety protocols. They also highlight the importance of practicing drills and reviewing safety plans regularly. By following these guidelines, healthcare staff can improve their ability to handle emergencies and protect themselves, patients, and visitors.

Steps for Healthcare Staff to Stay Prepared

Here are some practical steps that healthcare staff can take to stay prepared for emergencies:

1. Develop and Participate in Exercises and Training

    a. Healthcare facilities often conduct emergency exercises to help staff practice their response in their assigned areas. Participating in these exercises helps staff learn what to do in an emergency and stay familiar with safety procedures.

2. Review Safety Protocols Regularly

    a. Safety protocols are guidelines for how to respond to different emergencies. Staff should review and sign these guidelines when first hired and then review them yearly, so they know exactly what to do if something happens.

3. Communicate with Your Team

    a. In an emergency, communication is key. Talk with your team about what each person's role would be in a crisis. Knowing who to go to for help or direction can make responses quicker and more organized. This can be a short discussion with your shift before the week starts to throughout the workday when time permits.

4. Stay Aware of Exits and Safe Areas

    a. Knowing where exits and safe areas are located is important in case you need to escape or barricade. Healthcare staff should be familiar with the facility layout and know the safest routes.

Everyone Has a Role in Safety

"Always remember that safety is a shared responsibility." In a healthcare setting, every person has a role to play in maintaining safety. Whether you are a doctor, nurse, receptionist, cafeteria, or maintenance worker, being prepared and knowing what to do in any emergency is important. Working together and supporting each other creates a strong team that is ready for anything.

One quote that comes to mind for teams is this simple phrase:" Confidence over hesitation, and courage over fear." Safety is everyone's responsibility, and by following prepared guidelines, staying aware of surroundings, and participating in training, healthcare staff can make a real difference in protecting the lives of patients, visitors, and each other.

Preparedness in healthcare goes beyond having a plan; it's about fostering an emotionally safe environment where everyone is informed and ready to act in an emergency long before an attack happens. Preparedness is a state of readiness, appropriately assessing and choosing the best course of action, and successfully engaging it. Preparedness leads to good judgment.

We learned over 30 years ago that our core philosophy of "Treating People with Dignity by Showing Respect" can affect the point of impact, identify potential risks, increase the need to stay aware, and practice a proactive response mindset. Healthcare staff must be ready for anything.

Remember, safety is a shared responsibility. Every person has a role in keeping the healthcare environment safe. A team, by definition, is a group of individuals working together to accomplish the task at hand. With regular training, clear communication, and a culture of preparedness, healthcare teams can face emergencies with confidence and protect everyone in their care.

Chapter 2

What is an Active Assailant in Healthcare?

In any setting like hospitals, clinics, outpatient centers, and assisted living facilities, an "active assailant" is someone who enters the building intending to harm others. This person might have a weapon or behave in an aggressive and threatening way. Healthcare facilities are soft targets because of low to no defenses and the large number of vulnerable people concentrated in a small space.

Knowing how to recognize the warning signs of an active assailant is critical to helping keep everyone safe in any situation. Some specific behaviors and actions may signal that a person could become dangerous. For example, someone who is loudly raising their voice, using threatening words, or moving unusually or aggressively might be showing early warning signs. Additionally, people who act nervously refuse to answer simple questions, or seem hostile without reason could also be cause for concern.

"Sometimes people try so hard to blend in they stick out."

Being aware to these signs is a big part of staying safe. Healthcare staff are encouraged to communicate clearly and quickly if they notice any behavior that doesn't seem right. For instance, if a nurse or doctor sees a visitor acting in a way that feels uncommon or strange, or even intimidating, they should report it immediately to the correct authority in our organization. Unfortunately, many times, staff overlook behavior like this and chalk it up to the fact that this is the normal behavior for their job.

Quick communication helps prevent situations from escalating, meaning it can stop the person from becoming violent or causing harm to others.

Finally, reporting any unusual behavior, no matter how small it may seem, is strongly encouraged in healthcare settings. When staff members report their observations, they can help security or other trained personnel investigate the situation and, if necessary, take action to prevent harm. This proactive approach can prevent serious incidents and keep everyone in the facility, including patients, visitors, and staff, safer.

The SAFETY Formula to remember is simple:

The key to remembering is awareness, which aids in identifying. Identifying assists in prevention. Prevention is the partner to response.

Chapter 3

Staying Calm and Safe in a Healthcare Setting

In high-pressure healthcare situations, maintaining composure is crucial for effective decision-making and patient care. For example, during the COVID-19 pandemic, healthcare professionals faced unprecedented challenges that tested their resilience and ability to remain calm under pressure. Physicians, nurses, and technicians were constantly responding to emergencies, such as intubations, while managing their stress and fears. Despite the overwhelming circumstances, many found ways to stay composed, recognizing that their ability to remain calm directly impacted patient outcomes. They employed strategies like deep breathing and self-reflection to manage their stress before starting their shifts, understanding that a clear mind was essential for the critical decisions they had to make. [22]

This example illustrates the importance of healthcare workers staying calm during emergencies to think clearly and follow the necessary steps to ensure safety. By practicing techniques to manage stress and maintain composure, healthcare professionals can provide the best possible care, even in the most challenging situations.

[22] Lorenzini, 2023)

Staying calm is one of the most important things healthcare workers can do in an emergency. With a clear head, healthcare professionals can make quick, effective decisions. Calmness allows them to focus on the steps needed to keep themselves and others safe. Healthcare workers learn specific techniques to help them stay composed and in control, which is especially critical when they must act decisively to help others.

The Showtime Mindset

In all four programs, we share a tactic called the "Showtime Mindset."

Definition: Method to become emotionally, mentally, and physically prepared to respond appropriately to any situation.

Problem: Your internal mindset can negatively affect the outcome of an interaction.

Key Point: You must prepare in advance of any interaction to give the best professional representation of yourself.

Maxim: Imagine yourself stepping onto a stage to perform.

Before any interaction, particularly those that may involve conflict, establish a Showtime Mindset. Here's how:

- Clear your mind off other things that may be going on in your life; put aside any negative feelings or prejudices (i.e., ensure your prefrontal cortex isn't overwhelmed so your reasoning and social control are strong).

- Focus all your attention on your audience; see the world through their eyes.
- Project being their equal no matter who they are

Steps to Establish a Showtime Mindset

Here are the specific steps to establish a *Showtime Mindset*:

1. Say to yourself, "It's *Showtime*!" or a similar term that works for you.
2. "Stack your blocks." Adopt a confident posture by placing your head over your heart, shoulders over your hips, and hips over your knees.
3. Breathe deeply – in through your nose and out through your mouth.
4. Put on the appropriate facial expression for the situation.
5. Use positive self-talk (e.g., "I've got this." — "People are safer because I'm here now." ***I am going to survive!"***)
6. Step onto the stage (enter the situation)

Note: With the prevalence of cameras, every interaction is likely to be recorded. Therefore, from the moment you leave home, stepping onto a stage does not need to be imagined—it is reality. It is "*Showtime*."

In very stressful situations, the third step in the *Showtime Mindset* sequence can be accentuated with autogenic breathing—a technique for minimizing the effects of the body's "fight, fight, freeze, or freak out" mechanism. Here are the steps:

1. Inhale deeply through your nose for a count of four.
2. Hold your breath and slowly exhale.
3. Exhale through your mouth, with pursed lips, for a count of four.
4. Pause for a count of four.
5. Repeat to the extent possible.

Communication Alignment

Effective use of the *Showtime Mindset* requires all four elements of communication to be aligned with the situation (*Communication Alignment*). Just like an actor on stage, your proxemics, non-verbal, verbal, and para-verbal cues (tone of voice) must all send the same message.

Para-verbal refers to the aspects of communication that go beyond the actual words being spoken. It involves how something is said rather than what is said, including tone of voice, pitch, volume, speed, and intonation. Para-verbal communication can convey emotions, attitudes, and intentions, often influencing how a message is perceived by others. For example, a calm tone can indicate reassurance, while a loud and fast tone might signal urgency or frustration.

In high-stakes situations, you cannot overcome threatening non-verbal cues. Cues, like staring, toe-to-toe positioning, and aggressive posturing, with calm-sounding words and tone of voice.

When staff members stay calm, they are better equipped to handle tough situations and make sure everyone in the healthcare facility stays as safe as possible.

Example of applying Showtime for clinical staff in a dangerous situation:

Imagine you are on the 3rd floor of the hospital, making rounds. As you walk into a patient's room, you hear what appears to sound like 3 gunshots coming from the room you just left and provided care for. You quickly step into the closest room to get out of the hallway and say to yourself, "Showtime," you stack your blocks, take a few deep breaths in and out, say to put on your professional, confident face for the patient in the room you stepped into, you affirm to yourself, "I got this, I can do this, I am ready to keep myself and others safe." All these steps take 1-2 seconds.

Example of applying Showtime for healthcare security in a dangerous situation:

You receive a call from the emergency department about an unknown person who has entered the E.D. and is standing at the entrance, blocking people from entering the hospital. As you approach this unknown person, you observe that their clothing is torn, dirty, and frayed. As you get closer, they quickly turn in your direction, and you quickly notice they are bleeding on their left shoulder and holding a small firearm in their right hand.

You quickly step to their side, creating a little distance and putting your hands up, thinking to yourself, "Showtime." You stack your blocks, take a few deep breaths, and prepare yourself to engage with the individual confidently. You affirm, "I've got this," "I can do this," and "I'm ready to keep myself and others safe." These steps take just a few seconds, but they are essential in helping you remain composed and prepared for the situation.

Chapter 4

The Importance of Healthcare Safety Protocols

Healthcare facilities, like hospitals and clinics, have strong safety protocols that are reviewed and updated yearly. Regular updates ensure that protocols align with staff, locations, and patient populations, enhancing overall safety and preparedness.

A protocol is a set of established rules or procedures designed to guide actions in specific situations. It ensures consistency, safety, and efficiency by providing clear instructions on what to do, when to do it, and how to do it. Protocols are essential for maintaining order and achieving desired outcomes in various settings, such as healthcare, security, and emergency response.

One reason safety protocols are so important is that healthcare facilities often treat people who need extra care with movement restrictions. If there is an emergency, staff need to know how to respond quickly while keeping patients safe. These protocols can include procedures for escaping, options for moving patients, and emergency communications, which are ways to alert everyone if a dangerous situation arises.

For example, in emergencies such as an active assailant situation, staff and patients may need to think creatively to find safe escape routes.

Some patients may be unable to move or evacuate due to mobility issues or physical barriers. In cases where barricading is necessary, staff must choose a safer location based on specific criteria:

- The location does not provide a viable escape route.
- The danger is visible and approaching.
- The location offers an opportunity for self-defense.

If all three conditions are not met, then the chosen location is not the safest place to survive an active assailant attack.

In healthcare settings, barricading procedures might involve moving patients to safer areas and making sure doors to rooms and clinics are secure. Regularly reviewing and practicing barricading helps everyone remember the steps and stay prepared.

Another important part of safety protocols is maintaining secure entry points. This means making sure that entrances are monitored and only the right people can come in. These checks help find any areas that might need improvement, like adding locks, enhancing emergency lighting, or repairing and monitoring security cameras.

Healthcare protocols also include having clear communication plans. During an emergency, everyone must know what's happening and what to do. Staff need to communicate quickly and clearly to ensure that all patients, visitors, and other team members are informed and safe.

Every healthcare team member has a role to play in following and maintaining these protocols. By practicing these steps and understanding the procedures, they help create a safer environment for everyone. These protocols not only help in emergencies but also make healthcare staff feel more secure and confident every day.

Chapter 5

Managing Vehicle Emergencies in Healthcare Setting

Emergencies in healthcare settings are multifaceted and unpredictable. Among these, vehicle incidents—where a car crashes into a hospital or its premises can lead to significant challenges, including compromised safety, disruption of operations, and a chaotic environment. Such incidents can occur due to a variety of factors, including medical emergencies affecting drivers, human error, mechanical failures, or intentional acts of harm. In some cases, a vehicle incident may be part of a larger planned attack, escalating the threat level and requiring a comprehensive response.

This chapter explores how healthcare facilities can prepare for, respond to, and recover from vehicle-related emergencies, ensuring the safety and well-being of patients, staff, and visitors while maintaining operational continuity.

Types of Vehicle Incidents in Healthcare Facilities

Vehicle Incidents in healthcare facilities can range from accidental to intentional and include much bigger distractions or security risks. These include:

- Medical Emergencies: A driver experiencing a medical event (e.g., heart attack, seizure) may lose control of the vehicle.
- Human Error: Misjudging turns, mistaking the gas pedal for the brake, or speeding near entrances or drop-off zones can lead to accidents.
- Mechanical Failures: Brake failures or steering malfunctions, often compounded by environmental factors like slippery roads, poor visibility, or adverse weather conditions.
- Intentional Acts: A vehicle may be deliberately used as a weapon to target the hospital or its occupants. In some cases, a staged crash may serve as a diversion tactic, drawing emergency responders away while other malicious actions occur elsewhere.

Each scenario requires a specific response, but all benefit from preparedness and a clear understanding of protocols.

Critical steps for managing vehicle incidents can include but are not limited to managing immediate priorities. Moments following a vehicle incident are critical to minimizing harm and stabilizing the situation. Protect lives by addressing immediate dangers, such as evacuating affected areas and assisting the injured.

Assess the scene quickly and evaluate the extent of damage, number of injured individuals, and presence of secondary risks (e.g., fire, hazardous materials). Call for help and alert emergency services, including law enforcement, fire departments, and medical first responders, and be mindful that some of the professionals you are calling for help might need help themselves.

Make sure you identify potential threats in the hospital. Could this incident be related to the status of a patient, family member, or guest? Determine whether the crash is an isolated incident or part of a larger event. If this is accidental, focus on medical care and structural safety. If you assess this situation and find out it is intentional, remain vigilant for additional threats, such as armed assailants or secondary explosives.

Being prepared to take immediate steps to reduce risks and implement initial preventive measures can mitigate the risks and impact of vehicle incidents. Identify what physical barriers need to be installed, reinforced walls, or planters to protect vulnerable areas such as entrances, waiting rooms, and emergency departments.

Outside the hospital is another consideration, so do not forget traffic management and use clear signage, speed bumps, and designated drop-off/pick-up zones to control traffic flow. Manage your lighting and visibility to ensure adequate light around entrances and parking areas to reduce accidents.

In staff training and exercises, include vehicle crash scenarios in emergency training programs and train staff on recognizing potential threats, such as erratic driving behavior. It is, of course, important to coordinate with security teams to regularly review and update security protocols. Equip security personnel with the tools and training to manage vehicle-related incidents effectively.

Here is a quick acronym for responding to vehicle incidents in healthcare facilities: SECURE

- **S- Stabilize the Scene**- Protect lives by addressing immediate dangers (e.g., fires, injuries, or structural risks). Evacuate affected areas and secure the crash site to prevent further harm.
- **E- Evaluate the Incident**- Assess the situation, determine the extent of injuries and damage, and check for secondary threats (e.g., explosives, armed assailants).
- **C- Call for Help**- Notify emergency services, including police, fire, and medical responders. Communicate the situation, location, and any visible hazards.
- **U- Understand Potential Threats**- Investigate whether the incident is linked to a patient, family member, or external threat. Stay vigilant for diversion tactics or follow-up actions designed to cause additional harm.
- **R- Reduce Risks:** Take preventive measures by using barriers like bollards, planters, and reinforced walls to protect entrances. Implement effective traffic control with signage, speed bumps, and designated zones.
- **E-Educate and Equip Staff**-Train staff on recognizing and responding to vehicle incidents. Conduct emergency drills and update security protocols regularly. Using this acronym SECURE, simplifies the steps for responding to vehicle incidents in a healthcare setting, ensuring staff can act quickly and confidently to minimize harm, manage threats, and protect everyone involved.

The Risk of Premature Medical Response

A common concern in these incidents is that clinical staff may immediately assume the event is a medical emergency and rush to assist the injured driver or passengers. However, this could expose them to additional risks, such as an explosive device or an active assailant. Staff must assess the situation for potential threats before intervening.

By implementing security awareness into medical training, healthcare facilities can ensure that staff members prioritize both patient care and personal safety, reducing the risk of harm during high-risk incidents.

Chapter 6

Recognizing and Reporting Warning Signs

Recognizing early warning signs of potential violence can help prevent active assailant situations. In healthcare settings, signs such as heightened aggression, tense body language, or verbal threats may appear in patients, visitors, or staff prompt reporting of suspicious behavior allows for intervention before escalation.

When people act in ways that are rude or threatening, and no one stops them, those behaviors can start to feel normal. These actions, such as yelling, cursing, name-calling, and making threats, are known in our Vistelar Programs as "gateway behaviors." Gateway behaviors are actions that, if unaddressed, can escalate into more serious threats or violence. These include:

1. **Inappropriate Behavior:** Actions like disrespect, dismissiveness, or verbal hostility that create tension and disrupt order.
2. **Veiled Threats**: Indirect or implied threats, such as ambiguous comments suggesting harm or consequences.

3. **Direct Threats:** Clear statements of intent to harm, targeting individuals or groups.

4. **Violence:** Physical actions causing harm or fear, representing the culmination of unchecked gateway behaviors.

Addressing these behaviors early is key to preventing escalation and maintaining safety. Gateway behaviors, if not addressed early, can lead to more serious problems, including violence. If these behaviors go unchecked, they become acceptable, making it more likely that someone could get hurt emotionally or even physically.

The Role of a Social Contract

Instead of ignoring gateway behaviors, it's better to have a rule, called a "social contract," that makes it clear these actions are not acceptable. A social contract is an agreement or expectation of behavior. For example, in a pharmacy line, waiting quietly for your turn. If someone is too loud, other people feel comfortable telling them to be quiet. And if the person doesn't stop, the hospital staff will step in to remind them of the rules.

To keep places safe and respectful, organizations should create a social contract that includes:

1. A clear explanation of which behaviors are inappropriate (like shouting or making threats).

2. A policy of zero tolerance, meaning no one should accept these behaviors.

3. Training for staff to respond in the same way each time inappropriate behavior happens.

The Importance of Consistency

When rules are applied inconsistently, confusion and conflict can arise. As healthcare expert Joel Lashley from Vistelar states, "Inconsistency is the enemy of peace." Situations can easily become tense when expectations vary, as seen in these examples:

For example, situations can easily get tense if rules are not applied the same way every time, like in these examples:

1. *"Why do I need to wear a pass today? No one asked me yesterday!"*
2. *"Why can't I stay a little late? The person yesterday didn't say anything about visiting hours."*
3. *"Why am I being told to pay for a refill? The other cashier let me have one for free yesterday."*
4. *"Why are you telling me this when yesterday I already told them?"*

By enforcing clear, consistent policies, healthcare facilities can reduce conflicts and create a safe, respectful environment for everyone. A well-thought-out social contract ensures that expectations are understood and upheld, promoting a culture of safety and mutual respect.

Chapter 7

Response Strategies for Healthcare Settings

Response strategies for healthcare facilities include escape, barricading areas, and defending yourself as the last resort. Each strategy is designed to fit specific environments in healthcare, where patient mobility and medical needs may limit options. Staff should be familiar with the appropriate response for various scenarios. Having preplanned, practiced response in mind increases safety.

Stages of an Active Assailant Event (Event Timeline)

The timeline from when an active assailant first enters your facility to when the threat is terminated varies immensely. Each second counts. This is due to a myriad of factors, including your response. Your actions will depend on the stage of the active assailant incident.

Stage 1: Intruder Enters the Property

Stage 2: First Shot

Stage 3: First Injury

Stage 4: Police Notified

Stage 5: Police Arrive

Stage 6: Threat Terminated

Stage 7: Area Secured

Stage 1: Intruder Enters the Property

At this stage, the organization's workplace violence prevention preparation (or lack thereof) will be exposed. While there may be no direct comparison between the two, a debate can be made about the importance of reporting procedures for suspicious behavior, physical barriers, security cameras, and locks all in place. The time to prepare is now, by making sure that:

1. The organizational questionnaire is completed and current.
2. The workplace assessment checklist is completed and current.
3. Visual and physical deterrents are in place.
4. Your team treats everyone with dignity by showing respect.
5. Organizational sustainability training is up to date.

An example of an exercise for identifying the intruder on the property is:

1. Designate an unidentified staff member who dresses casually and carries a small backpack. The individual quickly enters the emergency department doors, walks past the desk to check in, stands in front of the elevator, pushes the buttons, enters the

elevator, and goes to a designated floor where security is standing by to escort them to the security office.

2. Allow 15 minutes to observe whether any staff member notifies security or approaches the person using the universal greeting.
3. Ensure all supervisors of effective departments are notified about the exercise to avoid any confusion or chaos.

Stage 2: First Shot

The first shot will create chaos and confusion. First, it is essential to confirm whether someone saw the shooter or heard gunfire and then notify the appropriate authorities accordingly.

An example is on January 26, 2016, when Naval Medical Center San Diego, near Balboa Park, experienced an active shooter incident. At approximately 8:00 AM Pacific Time, three shots were fired near Building 26 on the hospital campus. The Navy confirmed the gunfire but stated that no injuries were reported.

In response, the facility was placed on lockdown, and a shelter-in-place order was issued for all personnel and patients. San Diego police and military security forces conducted a thorough search of the premises. By 10:00 AM, authorities announced that the situation was resolved, and the lockdown was lifted. An unarmed individual was taken into custody, and no further threats were identified.

This incident underscores the importance of preparedness and effective response protocols in healthcare settings to ensure the safety of patients and staff during potential active assailant situations. [23]

Preparing for the first shot can be achieved through:

- Conducting department-wide training sessions
- Organizing section-specific exercises
- Holding quarterly training programs

An exercise to consider is to select a staff member that has been predetermined and hand them a 3 by 5 index card. The card says:

"This is a training exercise only. There is no immediate danger or threat to your safety. Please follow me to this room."

In this scenario, you are adjusting the curtain in a patient's room when you look out the window and see someone in the parking lot pull a handgun from their pocket and point it toward you. Consider the following steps of reporting and follow-up as your safety protocol:

1. Immediately call security.
2. Clearly describe what you have seen and provide the location.
3. Initiate your active assailant safety protocol.

This exercise is designed to ensure you are prepared to respond effectively in a real-life situation.

[23] (Garske, 2016)

Stage 3: First Injury

Once someone is injured, move them to a safe location before rendering aid so that you can perform first aid safely. Identify the type of injury and administer aid while keeping the individual conscious. If possible, call the authorities again to make sure they are responding. First injury actions include:

1. Immediate aid – This means to apply aid while still under duress, as while in the threatened area.

This includes inserting a finger into the wound to locate the pulsatile mass and applying compression or using a shoelace, phone charger, or another improvised tourniquet to stop the bleeding.

2. First aid- It is immediate care given to a person who has been injured or is suddenly ill before professional medical help is available. The purpose of first aid is to stabilize the individual's condition, prevent the situation from worsening, and save their life. This care can include simple actions like cleaning a wound, performing CPR, stopping bleeding, or using an automated external defibrillator (AED). First aid is not a substitute for professional medical treatment but serves as a critical first response. [24]

An exercise to consider is to select a staff member that has been predetermined and hand them a 3 by 5 index card. The card says:

---

[24] (American Red Cross, 2018)

1 As part of a training exercise, select a predetermined staff member and hand them a 3x5 index card that reads: "This is a training exercise ONLY. There is no immediate danger or concern for your safety. Please follow me to this room."

2 Inform them that during the escape scenario, they were shot.

3 Point to their right or left forearm and ask them to demonstrate how they would apply immediate aid and self-aid to the gunshot wound. Then, point to your forearm and instruct them to apply a tourniquet to your gunshot area, simulating the steps for assisting another person in a high-pressure situation.

Stage 4: Police Notified

Law enforcement response time varies greatly. Until the officers arrive, you and your co-workers are the immediate responders.

Note: When law enforcement arrives, their immediate focus will be on stopping the threat, which likely means engaging in gunfire. You should mentally prepare yourself for such violence. They will not assist victims in need of medical care until the threat is stopped. Their first goal is to stop the killing and then to stop the dying.

You should do the following:

1. Turn all cell phones on mute to manage noise.
2. Mark windows at your location to notify those on the outside that you are there. Signs should say "Help" or "Trapped room."

Training Exercise

This is a training exercise ONLY; there is no immediate danger.

1 Select a predetermined staff member and hand them a 3x5 index card that states: "This is a training exercise ONLY. There is no immediate danger or concern for your safety."

2 Lead the participant to the designated room.

3 Inform them that during an escape scenario, they saw a person in the lobby pull a firearm and start shooting.

4 Ask them to explain, in 60 seconds, the steps they would take based on the protocols. Including:

- Decide whether to escape, assist with patient movement, or barricade.
- Call from a secure location and provide:

1. Your name?
2. Exact location?
3. Suspect description?
4. Clear communication with police.

Stage 5: Police Arrive on Scene

In the United States, law enforcement agencies follow established protocols to respond effectively to active shooter incidents. The International Association of Chiefs of Police (IACP) provides guidelines for assessing threats and responding promptly during active attacks to minimize injury or loss of life. These protocols are designed to address various scenarios involving active assailants, including those using firearms, vehicles, explosives, or knives. [25]

Threat and keep you safe. They have been trained to address these situations. Following their directions will aid them in neutralizing the assailant as quickly as possible. This is one key reason to escape in the beginning to be able to provide on-scene information to police and possibly use escorts as most hospitals are like a maze.

Important Actions When Police Arrive:

1. Keep hands open and free of items.
2. Keep your hands out and visible.
3. Follow all law enforcement commands exactly as given.
4. Do your best to maintain your Emotional Equilibrium and perform Autogenic Breathing
5. Once outside the facility, go directly toward law enforcement with your hands visible

Actions to Avoid:

1. Do NOT point, move suddenly toward officers, or take other actions that may cause you to appear as a threat.
2. Do NOT scream or yell.

---

[25] (Active Attack*, 2025)

3. Do NOT engage in conversation with officers unless they are initiated by them.

4. Do NOT interfere with tactical officers' actions or touch them.

Coordination with Local Law Enforcement:

1. Know how they will respond.

2. Know how they will communicate with you during emergencies.

3. Establish mutual understanding for collaboration.

Training Exercise:

An exercise to consider is to select a staff member that has been predetermined and hand them a 3 by 5 index card. The card says: This is a training exercise ONLY.

This is a training exercise ONLY, and there is no immediate danger or concern for your safety. Begin by asking the participant to follow you to a designated room, then inform them they are escaping down a hallway when they see police entering. Instruct them to explain, within 60 seconds, the immediate steps they would take based on your protocols. These include removing anything covering their face or head, raising their open hands above their head to show they are unarmed, slowing their approach as they get closer to the officers, and moving to the sides of the hallway. Emphasize the importance of following all instructions completely, without hesitation, even if told or motioned to get on the ground.

Stage 6: Threat Terminated

Everyone must understand they are now safe. If you have not yet left the facility, stay in place. Move away from doors and exits. Show law enforcement your hands so they know you are okay and listen to every command. Conduct a wellness check of yourself and others.

If barricaded, wait in place until law enforcement has identified themselves and you confirm it is safe to show yourself. This should be covered in your training with your local authorities to bridge the response with your training. We recommend a safe word. An example of a safe word being used could be:

The officers announce their presence by saying, "This is Officer [Name] from the [Name of Agency]. Everything is okay. Is it safe to enter the room? Please respond with the safe word: 'Pineapple' if everything is secure." and the Officer would reply with "Cherries"

This approach ensures clear communication and provides a predetermined safe word to verify the authenticity of the response, reducing the risk of deception and prioritizing safety.

Training Exercise:

An exercise to consider is to select a staff member that has been predetermined and hand them a 3 by 5 index card. The card says:

This is a training exercise ONLY.

This is a training exercise only; there is no immediate danger or threat to your safety.

Begin by instructing the participant to follow you to a designated room, explaining that, in this scenario, they have chosen this room as their barricade location. Ask them to describe, within 60 seconds, the immediate actions they would take based on your protocols to secure and position themselves. These steps should include:

- Closing and securing the door.
- Turning off or adjusting the lights.
- Covering any windows.
- Using available items to barricade the door.
- Select the best position to take cover or prepare to disarm a potential threat near the doorway.

Stage 7: Area Secured

Once the facility is safe and the assailant is neutralized, turn your attention to yourself and identify any injuries or stress symptoms you are experiencing. You are safe and remind yourself that you are safe. When and if you can, continue to assist others. Remember that securing the facility will take several hours, and follow-up investigations will take weeks, maybe even months. At this stage:

1. **Follow Facility Chain of Command:** Adhere to the established protocol and leadership structure.
2. **Address Patients:** Assess whether patients need to be moved and prioritize their immediate care.

3. **Focus on Accountability:** Ensure patient records, conditions, and status are properly documented and tracked.
4. **Restore Normal Care Patterns:** Work to return patient care to standard routines as quickly as possible.
5. **Transport Patients or Support Items**: Coordinate the safe and timely transport of patients or necessary equipment to match previously relocated items.
6. **Manage Family Members**: Dedicate resources to communicate with and support family members of patients.
7. **Manage Public Messaging**: Control the flow of information to the public, especially family members and off-duty employees.

Additional Administrative Considerations:

1 Be prepared to set up a dedicated information line (or hotline) and broadcast the phone number via local media and social media sites to alleviate the incoming call volume to local dispatch centers.

2 Designate a media and press release person and location.

3 Designate a reunification location for family and friends once employees have been accounted for.

4 Set up an organization-wide after-action review and debrief.

5. Set up opt-out-only counseling and support services, including in-house support groups, access to chaplains or pastors, and professional counseling.

6. If certain areas of the hospital are closed off due to damage or a crime scene, what are your plans to deal with mass casualties and setting up alternate care sites within the hospital, on the campus, or elsewhere.

Training Exercise:

An exercise to consider is to select a staff member that has been predetermined and hand them a 3 by 5 index card. The card says:

This is a training exercise ONLY.

In this exercise, select a predetermined staff member and give them a 3x5 index card with the message: *"This is ONLY training exercise. There is no immediate danger or concern for your safety. Please follow me to this room."*

Once they are in the room, explain that, during their escape, they were shot. They now hear 6 to 8 gunshots followed by silence. Shortly after, the police announced "all clear" outside the room.

Instruct them to describe, within 60 seconds, the immediate steps they would take based on your protocols:

1. Move away from the doorway.
2. Listen carefully to the pre-arranged safe word to verify the rescuer's identity.
3. Remain still as the police enter the room.
4. Avoid rushing toward officers.

5. Keep their faces uncovered, raise their hands, and follow all instructions fully.

Stress the importance of staying calm by taking deep breaths and adopting the **"Showtime Mindset"** to remain mentally and emotionally prepared to respond appropriately in this high-stress scenario.

Chapter 8

Escape Barricade and Defend

The Run, Hide, Fight (RHF) program can be viewed as the first generation of armed assailant response programs, similar to how the A.L.I.C.E. program, initially designed for schools, served as a foundational model. In this context, EBD (Escape- Barricade - Defend) would represent the next generation, designed to better adapt to the unique needs of the healthcare community.

This progression highlights an evolution in both application and knowledge while still respecting the efforts of earlier programs. The development of police response strategies offers a useful analogy: Initially, law enforcement formed inner perimeters and waited for tactical teams, then moved to a four-man entry team, followed by waiting for backup officers, before finally reaching the modern approach of single-officer entry, seen as the most effective and swift method for confronting a shooter and saving lives.

Critics argue that single-officer entry is too risky, but as the saying goes, even a civilian would rush in to help. In this analogy, EBD represents the fourth generation or beyond, emphasizing the continued evolution and refinement of response protocols.

Ethical Considerations in Healthcare Response

Healthcare providers have a unique ethical obligation to protect the health and safety of not only their patients but also themselves.

Provision 3:

The nurse promotes, advocates for, and protects the rights, health, and safety of the patient [26]

Provision 5:

The nurse owes the same duties to self as to others, including the responsibility to promote Run, Hide, or Fight Programs. These provisions can create moral health and safety, preserve wholeness of character and integrity, maintain competence, and continue personal and professional growth" [27]

In high-risk situations, such as active assailant events, these ethical obligations may come into conflict. Healthcare professionals may be

[26] (American Nurses Association, 2025).
[27] (American Nurses Association, 2025)

forced to make impossible decisions, choosing between their own survival and continuing care for a patient.

The 2006 ANA position statement on risk and responsibility in providing nursing care states:

"Setting aside extraordinary circumstances under which nurses might choose to risk their lives, nurses do have a duty to tend to their well-being, not to place themselves in harm's way, or as the provision asserts, nurses have duties to self that ought to be observed."

At Vistelar, we hope that healthcare professionals are never put in a situation where they have to choose to risk their lives over the safety and treatment of patients. However, with the increased trends of violence and the continual escalation of active shooter events plaguing healthcare, the reality of a healthcare professional finding themselves in that situation is not impossible. [28]

"Even when law enforcement is present or able to respond within minutes, civilians often have to make life and death decisions, and therefore, should be engaged in training and discussions on decisions they may face." [29] According to statistics, active shooter events have been over before police have arrived [30]

The Need for an Alternative Model

[28] (Hospitals, Healthcare Workers Are "Soft Targets" for Shooters, 2024).

[29] (FBI Releases Study on Active Shooter Incidents Federal Bureau of Investigation, 2017).

[30] (Maximino, 2015)

The **Escape, Barricade**, and **Defend** curriculum gives healthcare professionals clear and direct-action steps that truly speak to the actions and decisions they will need to make in an active assailant situation. This book provides healthcare staff and their patients with the best possible chances of surviving such events.

Those actions should not be vague but rather be descriptive and evidence based. Evidence from the FEMA webpage states:

"The data show a clear pattern that those who took some form of decisive action at Virginia Tech fared much better than those who did not. Freezing or playing dead were not good options. [31]

Flaws in the Run, Hide, Fight Model

The 2012 **"Run, Hide, Fight"** program has been critiqued for two fundamental flaws:

1. **Failure to address the "Freeze" Response:** Critics argue that the model does not adequately consider the natural human tendency to freeze during high-stress situations, which can impede effective action. [32]

2. **Linear Approach:** The sequential nature of "Run, Hide, and Fight" may not align with the dynamic and unpredictable nature of active shooter events, potentially limiting individuals' ability to respond flexibly.

[31] (Protective Actions Research, 2025)
[32] (Wood, 2016)

In contrast, alternative models like "Escape, Barricade, and Defend" emphasize proactive strategies to overcome the fight-or-flight response. These approaches incorporate "when-then" thinking and mental crisis rehearsal training, encouraging individuals to mentally simulate various scenarios and plan their responses.

This mental preparation aims to reduce hesitation and improve decision-making under stress. [33]

It fails to recognize the caregiver's moral dilemma. The Escape, Barricade, Defend model works to overcome this by acknowledging its existence and has incorporated expert feedback from the healthcare profession.

If one examines the recommendations of actions to Run, Hide, and Fight and how this model fits within a healthcare organization. It does assist the healthcare worker in reconciling with the accepted level of responsibility to the patient. Run, Hide, or Fight Programs were never developed for the needs of healthcare organizations. They were meant for schools, concerts, and events without restrictions, physical limitations, or legal requirements that commonly apply to healthcare settings. They were developed as a general strategy at a federal level for a generalized program and disseminated from state to local assets to individual customer groups.

These programs are general and poorly address the needs of the employees in this customer base. These programs failed to address the

[33] (Gallegos, 2020)

responsibilities of health care workers to the patients in general, life-supporting medications, and treatments.

The **Run, Hide, or Fight** model fails to address caregiver responsibilities. Here are concerns at the policy and planning level.

Critical Unanswered Questions:

Facility Responsibilities:

1. What level of responsibility does the facility have to guarantee the personal safety of each staff member (or workers - contractors, volunteers, etc.) and patient?
2. What contingency plans do the facility have for personal safety in emergency situations?
3. Does facility policy prohibit staff from carrying weapons, thereby preventing them from defending themselves and patients?
4. Does the facility provide sufficient security measures to protect against external threats?

Healthcare Worker Responsibilities

5. What level of responsibility does a healthcare worker have in ensuring the personal safety of patients and visitors?
6. What is the Healthcare Worker's responsibility in ensuring their Safety?

In addition, a facility may be vulnerable to legal action if it fails to protect both staff and patients.

Traditional response models, such as Run, Hide, and Fight, fail to account for staff members who have physical limitations. This raises an important question:

- If a healthcare worker is unable to physically manage their safety, how does this impact their ability to keep others safe?
- Escape routes, hiding places, and defensible positions are not universal across all departments.
- Staff may lack adequate resources to protect themselves and their patients in high-risk situations.
- There may be no clear policies outlining staff, visitor, and patient responsibilities during an attack.

Additional questions to ask are: there are competencies to refine or a performance checklist during your program? Does your program share policies for the direction of patients and visitors when they are running or fighting during the attack? Do the patients and visitors have guidance on what to do during an active shooter event?

There is no independent guidance such as instructions in orientation, signs, posters, or wall directions for patients and visitors to act in situations where time is a primary factor for survival.

There is no consideration for integrating the running, hiding, or fighting of patients and visitors into the efforts of the staff. There is a distinct lack of coordination. This raises further critical questions:

1. What is the staff's responsibility to coordinate efforts between staff, patients, and families?
2. What is the chain of command structure in the facility during an event?
3. What is the requirement of a patient or visitor to comply with the staff? If staff gives directions to patients and visitors.

Additional Policy Gaps

- What is the staff's role in coordinating efforts between patients, families, and visitors?
- What is the healthcare worker's responsibility in managing medical records, medications, and lifesaving treatments for patients while evacuating or in emergency situations?
- What is the reconciliation with state requirements of licensed personnel of management of concerns of records, medications, and lifesaving treatments?
- Are allowances made in these circumstances of emergencies or force of nature?
- Does staff understand what their roles are in regards to escaping the area during an active shooter attack while responsible for patients?

- Define abandonment per ***your*** state, and how does this affect the emergency response of the staff?

- What defines an emergency or force of nature? Does an active assailant emergency parallel duties, responsibilities, and liabilities of staff relations to differently named disasters?

- To what degree are allowances made for HCWs (health care workers) who are not in the immediate area of the event? Are all events considered facility or area-wide events?

The Need for Comprehensive Training

A quote from Paul Carter, a Vistelar Trainer with over 3 decades of healthcare experience, shared:

"In over 30 years of nursing, the most detailed exposure of this type of training a nurse received in an active shooter program was generally a 1-page paper, concealed in a stack of other disaster plans, briefs, that discussed concepts, with no actionable steps, or guidance. Most of these were decidedly anti-helpful."

With the safety and well-being of our patients and staff being of utmost importance, I respectfully wonder why there seems to be a lower priority placed on training that could help protect them in critical situations.

Lessons from Military Medical Training

Paul Carter served as a U.S. Army Active Duty Nurse for 15 years before transitioning to U.S. Army Special Operations Forces. His role shifted from traditional patient care to tactical healthcare operations, where he worked in high-risk combat zones and provided on-the-ground medical support in volatile environments.

He survived over 60 combat engagements and deployments in the Middle East. He returned to being an active-duty nurse and worked to support a program called the Joint Readiness Training Center (JRTC) at Fort Polk, Louisiana. The JRTC is a program to provide the last opportunity for a dress rehearsal for units that are being deployed into a combat zone. A key focus of his work was preparing medical personnel to handle mass casualty incidents under direct threat.

Strengthening the Purpose of Military Training

At first glance, combat-zone medical training may seem unrelated to civilian healthcare environments, but key lessons from military preparedness can directly apply to hospital security. Reserve units are required to attend monthly drills at a military hospital as care supplements and must leave their normal drill responsibilities and form a deployable a functional military hospital. These military field hospitals receive casualties from both friendly and hostile groups, under conditions where security is not always guaranteed. Everyone is treated, and no one may be turned away. The areas that the hospitals were physically located in were not necessarily secure, making them vulnerable to external threats, much like civilian healthcare facilities. As part of their security training, medical units participate in simulated attacks, which frequently involve an active assailant scenario. These drills mirror the real-world risks healthcare workers face, where medical teams may be caught in the middle of violence while tending to patients. Despite extensive training, Paul Carter observed that even armed reservists, who had met Army Physical Fitness Standards and completed rifle qualifications struggled to effectively respond when operating in a medical environment.

Time and time again, Paul said he witnessed firsthand the impact of this event in the area. He observed the reactions of both staff and patients, even after briefings were provided and training was conducted. Please note that these students have met a physical standard by successfully passing their Army Physical Fitness Tests, qualifying them for deployment.

Each time these training simulations occurred, he observed close to 100% of casualties of personnel and patients in the primary attack area, where the active assailant first engaged. Additionally, there were another 50% casualties in secondary areas of impact. All of this occurred within the first 3 minutes of the simulation.

Depending on the physical access, communications, and ability of staff to defend themselves, the active assailant in the simulation would continue until the attack is neutralized by the staff, which took another 12-15 minutes. Due to the MILES gear (Multiple Integrated Laser Engagement System), is a training system used by the military to simulate combat situations. It functions similarly to laser tag. Combatants wear vests and helmets equipped with sensors that detect hits from laser 'bullets' fired by weapons equipped with laser emitters. This system provides immediate feedback on the effectiveness of engagement tactics and maneuvers, allowing soldiers to conduct force-on-force or force-on-target exercises that mimic real combat scenarios without the risk of injury, is gear used in the simulation, this accounted for no collateral damage or casualties. The assailants' fire would have easily penetrated the tent walls, striking equipment or people. Paul's opinion is that real-life scenario with a similar setup, the casualties would have been much higher.

If the number of staff in the field hospital was perhaps 85 during a given point in time, Paul said he observed, on average, 30-50 casualties from the exercise. Every MILES hit was counted as a fatality for the simulation. The assailant simply walked through the hospital area and shot everyone they saw, acting as an untrained assailant until they were eventually eliminated.

A real-life example occurred at Fort Hood, Texas on November 5, 2009. Major Nidal Hasan, a U.S. Army psychiatrist, carried out a mass shooting that resulted in 13 deaths and 32 injuries. [34]This incident stands as one of the deadliest mass shootings on a U.S. military base. For comprehensive information on this event, you may refer to the following sources listed in our reference section. Paul closely reviewed what occurred during these training events and the safety of healthcare workers and patients. Discovering that safety and care do not have to be exclusive to each other.

An Escape, Barricade, Defend mindset presents goals and actions more clearly and is relevant to the end state of increasing survival

[34] Sullivan, 2011)

opportunities and managing liabilities with their rifles and shot (simulated, of course) at everyone they saw. It should be noted that the "assailants" did not use any of their specialized training to sneak up on or attack the staff, they simply walked in and started shooting like an untrained assailant would.

People remain flexible and may need to switch between escape, barricade, and/or defend" as the incident evolves or as they move through the facility to escape.

Guidance from Homeland Security and Nursing Experts

The U.S. Department of Homeland Security's 2008 publication, **Active Shooter:** *How to Respond,* provides guidance on preparing for and responding to active shooter situations. It emphasizes that individuals should take action against an active shooter only as a last resort when their lives are in imminent danger. [35]'Taking action against the active shooter. As a last resort, and only when your life is in imminent danger, will you attempt to disrupt and/or incapacitate the active shooter. The recommended actions include:

1. Acting as aggressively as possible against him/her.
2. Throwing items and improvised weapons
3. Yelling
4. Committing to your actions

[35] (Active Shooter How to respond, 2008)

According to Walden and colleagues (2021), "Each nurse in an active threat situation must assess their level of risk and personal capabilities and make a personal choice to either prioritize their safety by temporarily leaving their patients or to remain and accept the high risk of personal injury or death at the hands of the shooter."[36]

Escape, Barricade, and Defend: A Smart Approach

Like other active assailant preparedness programs, **Escape, Barricade, Defend** is an option-based active assailant response strategy, which is the most effective way to save lives.

Below are a few skills that will be taught by Vistelar in an actual training session and are not discussed in detail here. For example:

Escape

1. **Understanding our Unified Conflict Management Systems,** it starts with knowing what to do BEFORE these incidents occur. Our Non-escalation, De-escalation, and Crisis Management (NE DE CM) Framework prevents such incidents from escalating at the point of impact.
2. Risk Assessment Training, Key skills include:

- Situational awareness (proxemics, scanning, and sight lines)
- Cover vs. concealment
- Environmental assessment (doors, walls, and escape routes)

[36] (Walden et al., 2021)

3. Skills trained in identifying "safer" escape routes, knowing how to get out of where you are, where to go, and what to do when you get there.

4. The identification of a **"safer place"** and choosing a place where one can still see danger coming, can still exit from and can defend if needed.

5. Identifying how to more effectively navigate stairs, hallways, and open areas.

6. Patient considerations are to survive first and protect next.

    a. If a patient cannot be moved or resources are unavailable, consider turning off lights and noise to make the room appear empty.

    b. Use commercially available door wedges or lock brace devices to create barricade options.

    c. This strategy may be feasible if the patient can place the device, a family member is present, or a staff member can lock themselves in with the patient.

    d. Ensure the barricade method is practical and does not compromise the patient's safety or care.

7. Safe approach and surrender to law enforcement.

8 Managing others dealing with emotional trauma.

9. Immediate, self, and first aid procedures for rendering aid for injuries and gunshot wounds.

Barricade

Skills trained in:

a. Selecting the safest room criteria.

b. Identification of doors, locks, and latches.

c. Identification of windows and types of glass

d. Pre-staged objects are commercial products, which can be purchased and staged for use.

e. How to barricade various types of doors.

f. In-room placement for cover and how to avoid the impact area

g. In options when barricading is not an option

h. Teamwork for working together under stress

Defend

1. Skills trained in:

a. Conducting risk assessments

b. Conducting threat assessments

c. Identifying preferable items and weapons of opportunity

d. Selecting engagement and positioning

e. Considerations for identifying criteria for weapons of opportunity, knowing what you are trying to do with the item, taking into consideration the distance it will keep you from the attacker, and considering how much effort it will take to wield it effectively

f. Creating teamwork and communication

g. Focused training on ambushing the attack

h. Disarming options for individual or team contact.

Chapter 9

Escape Techniques and Assisting Others

In a healthcare setting, knowing how to escape safely during an emergency is crucial. When facing a threat, such as an active assailant, escaping quickly is often the safest option. Here are techniques for escaping, helping others, and navigating safely through different areas.

Escape: Moving to Safety

It is important to plan for the escape of patients with limited mobility is essential in active assailant situations." Identify escape routes that are wheelchair accessible or suitable for individuals using walkers or gurneys. Including elevators and ramps in evacuation plans but avoid elevators in case of fire or structural risks. The patient may have physical limitations, which limit their mobility. If elevators are unavailable, moving these patients becomes extremely difficult. In addition, medical equipment and assistive devices, which are already challenging to transport under normal conditions, become even harder to manage in a crisis. Consider moving patients around within the same ward or floor to the most defensible position and use commercial barricade tools into the largest and strongest room available.

Use assistive devices wisely and secure walkers and wheelchairs for quick movement. Assign staff or volunteers to assist those with mobility challenges. Before an emergency occurs, pre-assign helpers by pairing individuals with limited mobility with a trained staff member or caregiver to ensure their safety and support during the crisis.

Conduct drills to ensure staff are familiar with assisting these individuals safely and quickly. If escaping is too difficult, identify nearby rooms that can serve as safe barricade locations. Ensure these areas are stocked with emergency supplies and communication tools.

Prioritize communication and use clear, calm instructions to guide individuals with mobility challenges. Ensure they know where to go and who will assist them. Prepare specialized equipment in areas needed like I.V. poles, walkers, and chairs, and position other transport aids readily available in critical areas.

Train staff on how to use these tools effectively. Accounting for standard hospital transport tools such as gurneys, wheelchairs, and hospital beds in healthcare settings and ensure gurneys are mobile and have clear pathways for movement. Plan for areas where patients can be moved safely without compromising their medical care.

Each department serves a diverse range of patient demographics, requiring tailored training and equipment to effectively respond to emergencies. It is crucial to conduct training at the department level to ensure staff are equipped to understand the specific needs of their patient population and implement appropriate Escape or Barricade procedures.

Escaping means moving yourself and others to a safe place away from danger. This process is often called "getting off the 'x,'" which means leaving the area where the threat is. You should plan escape routes, know obstacles along each route, and consider your physical abilities.

Choose an escape route within your abilities. For example, if you have an injury, avoid routes that involve stairs or climbing. Find a secure place to go once you're outside. Look for locations where you can hide safely, see danger approaching, ability to defend form this location, and have another way to escape if needed. Avoid rushing to unsafe spots.

The mind picture that this creates is a deliberate action with a goal in mind, Staying focused in this way maintains a sense of purpose while under duress and helps to prevent a panic state.

Avoid main entrances when planning escape routes, avoid the main entrances when possible. The main entrance should never be the only option. Look for alternative exits, like emergency doors or windows. Law enforcement officers might direct you to exit a specific way, so keep your hands visible and follow their instructions carefully.

Escape vs. Lockdown

Escaping is generally faster and safer than locking down. If you can't create a safe barricade or defend yourself, escaping should be your top priority. Leave behind belongings to move as quickly as possible. If you hear a pause in gunfire, it may mean the assailant is reloading. This is often the best time to escape.

When moving through hallways or open areas, follow these techniques to stay safe:

1. Move as a group, on the balls of your feet to reduce noise.

2. If you stay close together in a group stagger your positioning never escape in a group larger than three due to the larger target you create. If in hallways, stagger your line by placing a hand on the shoulder of the person in front. This technique keeps everyone steady and aware.

3. Rounding the Corner, Slicing or Cutting the Pie. When approaching a corner, move to the opposite side of the hallway to improve your view. Use the physical edge of the corner to hide behind for cover before stepping out into the next hall, exposing yourself.

4. Stay Low and Move Fast. In open areas, move in a zig-zag pattern to make it harder for an attacker to target you. Run from cover to cover when possible and change directions every few steps.

5. The Laser Rule: Imagine an attacker pointing a gun like a laser at you. Running in a straight line makes you an easy target. Zig-zagging makes it harder for them to aim.

6. Use the mantra "I am up, he sees me, I am down." Run a few steps, then crouch or lie down. Repeat until you reach safety.

Moving in Stairwells

When navigating stairwells, stay near the wall side of the railing. This keeps you out of sight and gives you extra protection. Avoid the middle area of the stairwell. Move quickly and watch for obstacles, like doors or debris. Carefully manage your balance and forward momentum. When you need to move quickly, do not do it in such a way that you cannot slow to peak around corners or back up quickly if needed. Backing backward upstairs can be difficult, especially if your legs are already getting tired, or you are moving forward quickly.

Window Escapes

If you cannot use a door, consider escaping through a window. To meet some of the many compliance considerations a hospital deals with hospital windows may have to meet requirements dealing with things, such as tempered or laminated glass, impact-resistant, fire-rated glass, energy-efficient multi-pane windows, anti-glare coatings, and blast resistance that can make breaking through them very difficult. Knowing which windows are low enough for you to access and climb through, may open wide enough to get through, or that you are physically capable of breaking through and moving through with a reasonable chance of doing so safely. Ensure you can physically move to your escape location after you are through.

Here's how:

1. Attempt to open the window first
2. Then pry it open if possible

3. As a last resort, break the window.
    - Tap the glass first to crack it
    - Break it and sweep the window frame for any loose glass
    - Rake the debris from the window by using an object
    - Then escape
4. Place tape or a curtain over the glass to prevent shattering. Rake the glass and sharp debris away. Use something other than your bare hand to sweep away broken glass from the frame.
    - Heavy clothing
    - Mousepads
    - Curtains
    - Small Rugs
5. Use Items for Protection. Lay books or other objects over any remaining glass on the windowsill to avoid cuts.
    - Try using heavy clothing
    - Loose Carpet
    - Floor mats

Safe Rescue Techniques

Some people may need help escaping, either due to injury, fear, or disorientation. Remember to ask them if they need your help. In crises, touching too aggressively can trigger tragic results. Here's how to assist:

1. **Assisted Escort:** This technique is for helping someone who may be in shock or unable to move alone.

    - Approach calmly, avoid loud sounds, and keep a bit of distance until they acknowledge you.

    - Place your hand on your partner's back for support and guide them by gently wrapping your arm around their shoulders.

    - Crouch slightly to create stability and move slowly to a safe location.

2. **Follow the Leader Escort:** If you're moving with children or small frail and fragile patients or a group, use the follow the Leader method. Have patients hold the hips or belt of the staff in front. The rear staff holds the shoulders of the patient, keeping everyone together.

3. **Fireman's Carry:** For someone injured but close in size to you, use the Fireman's Carry:

    - Bend down, place your shoulder at their abdomen, and pull their leg over your shoulder.

- Support their hand over your other shoulder and stand up, allowing one hand to stay free.

4. **Side Buddy Carry:** This is for someone who can move but needs support on one side.

    - Stand next to them, supporting their back with your arm.
    - Hold their belt or hip to stabilize and move them with their weight on their uninjured leg.

5. **Body Drags:** If lifting is not an option, use body drags to move injured people.

    - Upper Body Drag: For lower-body injuries.
    - Cross their arms in their lap, reach under their armpits, and hold their wrists.
    - Bend your knees, lift, and use your legs to pull them to safety.

6. **Lower Leg Drag:** For upper-body injuries:

    - Cross their arms over their body.
    - Stand between their legs, hold their ankles, and drag backward or forward, depending on the situation.

7. **Sheet or Blanket Drag:** If the person is injured or too heavy to move alone

    - Lay the person on a sheet or blanket or even a jacket.

Wrap them securely and drag them out of the dangerous area. Stay Calm and Follow Instructions in Rescues

When you first encounter law enforcement, and their identity is confirmed, follow these steps.

1. **Cooperate fully:** Rescuers may not know who the threat is, so cooperate fully, even if they ask to search or handcuff you. Your priority is survival, so remain calm and allow them to work through their process. They do not know that you are not the shooter and may act cautiously to ensure safety. Complying fully helps them assess the situation quickly. Avoid arguing, correcting them, or speaking loudly, as this could cause confusion or delays. Law enforcement must quickly rule out multiple people as threats, often with limited information, so do not distract or slow them down in any way.

2. Do not run unless instructed: Follow all instructions carefully. Stay in place to avoid being mistaken for a threat.

3. Proceed to the Designated Safe Area: Once you have escaped the threat area, head to the designated safe area as directed. Be evaluated and help evaluate others for wounds and injuries. Assist the wounded and manage the mental and emotional state of all survivors. Do not speak to the press. Do not post on social media. Do not communicate with outsiders other than quick text to family of "I'm safe, will call when I can, I love you". You need to stay accounted for. You may be needed when the building is clear to assist with casualties, evaluate survivors, and re-establish

care for patients. You will be asked to provide statements, debrief, and provide information about last seen patients, family, or staff. You may be asked to identify casualties whom you know or be asked to fulfill other varied responsibilities. Lastly, you will receive instructions on how to guide response personnel outside in managing security and coordinating outside personnel.

One of the main reasons these tactical movements are critical is the need to move an injured person to safety before you can render aid during an active assailant event. Within a hospital, the inability to move or relocate injured patients with mobility limitations, presents unique challenges. Here are key considerations and concerns to address:

1. **Prioritization of Patient Safety**

   - **Assessment of Threat:** Assess how immediate the threat is to patients in locations who cannot be moved. Use hospital communication systems to understand the assailant's location and determine if it's safer to shelter in place with vulnerable patients.

   - **Communication:** Normal Communication may be ineffective. Determine whether patients will have access to acceptable alternative communication tools.

2. **Barricading Measures**

    - **Securing the Area:** Lock doors, close curtains, and turn off lights to make the area appear unoccupied. Avoid unnecessary noise and movement. Do not draw attention to your location.

    - **Emergency Equipment:** Ensure access to emergency supplies (such as oxygen tanks, extra IV bags, and other essential medical supplies) to sustain patients in place.

    - **Patient Comfort and Quiet:** If possible, keep patients calm to avoid drawing attention.

    - **Door Barricading:** Have predetermined methods to barricade and secure doors that cannot be locked.

3. **Staff and Patient Safety Training:**

    - **Safety Procedures:** Staff should be trained on "Escape, Barricade, and Defend" protocols, modified for healthcare environments, so they know how to manage people who are mobility impaired.

    - **Non-Physical Barriers**: If physically hiding is not possible, create barriers using furniture or equipment to obstruct access.

    - **Cover vs. Concealment:** Remember that cover physically protects you from bullets, and concealment hides you from the attacker's vision.

4. **Alternative Safety Precautions**

    - **Room Preparation:** Make use of rooms designed for containment in emergencies, such as those with secure locking mechanisms or rooms within critical care areas that can be locked. What rooms are identified as an escape option? The staff can pre-identify "safe" locations to give options for escaping staff based on their location and circumstances. Develop a list of critical requirements to investigate escape locations and prepare strategies for escape.

    - **Critical Equipment Access**: Ensure that essential devices, such as heart monitors, ventilators, and life-support equipment, are set up to operate autonomously in the event that staff must temporarily distance themselves from patients.

5. **Psychological Support**

    - **Emotional Stabilization:** Help reassure patients to prevent unnecessary movement and distress.

- **Remote Communication:** Utilize intercom systems or two-way radios to maintain contact with isolated patients whenever possible, ensuring they receive clear instructions and support. Additionally, consider the appropriate use of personal cell phones, as there is a high likelihood that staff, patients, and family members may have their devices with them. If permitted by local policy, personal cell phones can be used to facilitate communication through a central control system, such as 911 operators or other designated emergency communication hubs, following the established response plan for the area.

6. **Post-Incident Considerations**

    - **Triage and Medical Support:** Develop a rapid triage protocol for addressing any injuries from the incident and for identifying patients needing urgent care. This protocol is not an ER triage note. It is more like a pre-facility mass casualty sorting to determine the number and severity of injuries to direct the resources of care.
    - **Emotional and Psychological Care:** Ensure that mental health resources are readily available for both patients and staff after the incident, especially for those who were immobilized. Individuals acutely affected by stress or anxiety can be directed to immediate resources balanced with those with physical injuries. All others can be directed to debriefing and mental health resources for immediate resourcing and long- term support.

In active assailant situations, healthcare facilities must implement comprehensive emergency planning to balance patient safety with medical care. Preparing for patient immobility requires advanced planning, staff training, and clear communication protocols to minimize risks and improve outcomes.

Chapter 10

Top 10 Considerations for Barricading in Healthcare Settings

In healthcare settings, barricading is an important safety step in emergencies. Knowing how to create effective barriers can help protect staff, patients, and visitors. Here are some important things to think about when it comes to barricading in a healthcare environment.

1. **Identifying secure areas for barricading:** Identifying secure areas for barricading is critical to saving lives. Identify the safest rooms or spaces for barricading as part of the planning process. A set of criteria can be developed, and a selection of potential rooms can be made with the facilities engineers who manage the physical structure of the building. Rooms with solid doors and no windows are ideal because they provide protection and are harder to break into. In healthcare, suitable barricade locations include patient rooms, supply closets or administrative offices. Knowing which rooms are safest can save time during an emergency.

2. **Use available objects to block doors:** In healthcare facilities, there are often many objects that can be used to block doors. Hospital beds, cabinets, chairs, and carts can all help create

barriers. Learn how to use nearby objects to secure doors. If you are in a patient's room, use the bed or furniture to create a strong block. Additionally, third-party commercial barricade devices, such as portable lock brace devices, can be used to reinforce doors and prevent unauthorized access.

3. **Understanding different door types**: Not all doors are the same. Some doors swing inward, while others swing outward, affecting how you can barricade them. For example, it's easier to block a door that swings inward by placing furniture in front of it. Learning about the types of doors in your facility and practicing different barricading methods can make a big difference in an emergency.

4. **Knowing how locking mechanisms work:** Make sure you know how to lock different types of doors. In some cases, doors may have electronic locks, keypads, or manual locks. Knowing how each lock works allows you to quickly secure a room. If certain doors cannot be locked, focus on barricading them effectively with objects or furniture. Keyed locks may only allow access to staff who have those physical keys, and any door that services people (not stored) may have a badge-keyed electronic lock that can allow access for staff. Keep in mind that these doors are automatically unlocked in the circumstances of a loss of power or if the fire alarm is activated. A third-party barrier device may be needed to ensure barricade.

5. **Using door handles for barricades:** Door handle designs influence how a door can be secured. L-shaped handles allow for barricading using objects such as the leg of a chair or a metal pole, which can prevent the door from being opened. Understanding these small but significant details can provide additional barricading options in areas where traditional methods may not be feasible.

6. **Use belts, ropes, and extension cords**: If heavy furniture is unavailable, alternative barricading options include using belts, ropes, or extension cords. Tying these around door handles and securing them to fixed objects can help prevent the door from being opened. This method may be useful when you are in a small room with few objects. You may have to disconnect the cables from television or other electronic devices.

7. **Using Fire Hoses to Secure Doors:** Use a fire hose segment over the pneumatic door closer to the inside of a door, if possible. Contact your local fire department to ask for short sections of used fire hoses for this purpose.

8 **Positioning People Away from Doors and Windows:** Once a barricade is in place, it's important to position everyone in the room away from doors and windows. This reduces visibility and keeps everyone safer. Keeping individuals low to the ground and quiet can further enhance safety. Windows should be covered using curtains, blinds or any available material to block the view inside the room. In the patient's room, positioning yourself

closer to the door and on the ground is safer than in the back of the room, where bullets land if shots are fired.

9. **Practice barricading procedures regularly:** Practice is essential in a healthcare setting. Staff should practice barricading procedures so that, during an emergency, they know exactly what to do. Healthcare facilities can schedule regular drills to ensure everyone is comfortable with the process. Practicing reduces panic, improves reaction time, and increases overall safety during real-life emergencies.

10. **Communicating with others and knowing when to Exit:** Listen carefully to instructions from law enforcement or security personnel before leaving the barricaded area. If you must exit before help arrives, move quietly, keep hands visible, and ensure the area is safe before proceeding. New staff members should be familiarized with potential escape routes in their assigned locations to improve response efficiency during an emergency.

11. **Be Prepared for Long Waits:** During training, barricading exercises may last only 15 minutes, but in a real emergency, you may need to stay in place for hours. If you're barricaded during an emergency, you may need to stay put for an extended period. Make sure to have basic supplies, like water and first-aid kits, available in barricade areas if possible. Staff can also plan to have quick access to emergency supplies in case of long waits.

12. **Know when and How to Exit:** Knowing when it's safe to exit is just as important as setting up a barricade. Listen carefully to

any instructions from law enforcement or security personnel. If you must leave before help arrives, make sure to move as quietly and safely as possible with nothing in your hands, checking that it is truly safe to do so. It takes only a few minutes to walk a new staff member through some important facts about a new area they are working in.

Chapter 11

Barricading Tactics in a Healthcare Environment

In emergencies, if you cannot escape, the next best option is to barricade the door to delay an attack and buy yourself additional life-saving time to think and defend yourself if necessary.

Barricading means blocking entry to your location so a threat cannot reach you. Unlike just hiding, barricading is about creating a strong barrier that protects you and others. Here's how to do it effectively in a healthcare setting.

What is Barricading?

When you barricade, you set up a physical block to prevent an assailant or threat from entering. Simply hiding out of sight is not enough; the purpose of barricading is to make it difficult or impossible for someone to break into your space.

Avoid the common mistake of thinking that piling random objects behind the door will effectively block entry. A loose stack of items may not provide the necessary support or strength to prevent an intruder from opening the door.

Effective Barricading Requires:

Effective barricading requires securing the door with sturdy, heavy objects or using a dedicated door lock brace or wedge that can withstand pressure and force. Simply blocking the door with random items won't create the level of security needed in an active threat situation.

To make a secure barricade, you will need enough weight or leverage to stop anyone from opening the door. In some cases, you may have to use furniture, body weight, or other objects to build this barrier.

The Power of Weight

Think of the barricade as a barrier made up of many objects. If the attacker weighs about 200 pounds, you may need twice that weight on the door's other side to keep them out. Heavy items like desks, cabinets, and shelves make excellent barricades because they add a lot of weight. If heavy furniture is not available, use door wedges or even ropes to help reinforce the barricade. When possible, stack items tightly together to make them harder to move.

Step-by-Step Barricading for Different Doors

Inward-swinging doors are easier to barricade because they open toward you. To secure this type of door:

1. Place heavy objects close to the door, such as desks, chairs, or filing cabinets.
2. Push the items together, packing them tightly to prevent movement if force is applied from the outside.

3. If you don't have enough weight, use body weight by pressing yourself or others against the objects. However, be aware of your position as the shooter may shoot through the door.

Outward-swinging doors are harder to barricade since they open away from you. To secure these:

1. Use objects larger than the door frame, like a long table or bookshelf.
2. Tie off the door with a belt, cord, or rope around the door handle to another heavy object.
3. If the door has a hydraulic arm, place a piece of used fire hose over the arm so it cannot open. Contact your local fire department to request short pieces of used fire hose for this purpose.

Using Additional Reinforcements

If you lack heavy objects, you may need to be creative with the tools around you.

1. **Door Wedges:** Wedges are small pieces of wood or rubber that can be pushed under the door to keep it shut. A door wedge under an inward-swinging door can make it harder to push open. Be sure the wedge does not stick out on the other side, or the attacker will know you are barricaded.
2. **Coins or Small Items:** Coins or small items can be wedged at the top of the door to create extra friction. Be careful not to place

coins around locks or latches, as this can weaken the door's structure.

3. **Super Glue:** Super glue can temporarily seal a door closed, though this will prevent you from exiting through that door later. This option is best if you have no other way to secure the door.

4. **Books:** The front or back hard cover of books can be jammed into the top, side, or bottom of the door

Choosing and Positioning Objects

When choosing objects to barricade with, remember to:

1. **Use Solid, Heavy Items:** Desks, bookshelves, and filing cabinets are ideal.

2. **Keep Books on Shelves:** Books add weight, making it harder for the attacker to push through.

3. **Push Items Together:** Tightly packed items are much more challenging to move or breakthrough.

4. **Watch for Sharp Corners:** In a healthcare environment, ensure items like metal carts do not pose a safety hazard for people nearby.

Creative Barricading Ideas

If traditional barricading items are unavailable, think creatively:

1. **Moveable objects like bedside tables and carts:** In patient rooms, bedside tables and rolling carts can be moved quickly to create a barrier.

2. **Medical Equipment:** IV stands, wheelchairs, and even large medical supplies can be placed against the door to add weight.

3. **Curtains:** Heavy hospital curtains, if they reach the floor, can be tucked into door frames to create a seal.

Building a Temporary Barricade

Remember that all barricades are temporary. They're meant to delay entry, not necessarily prevent it entirely. The longer it takes for someone to break through, the more time you have to plan your next steps or wait for help.

Staying Out of Sight

While setting up your barricade, it's essential to stay out of sight:

1. **Avoid Visible Positions:** Stand to the side of the door while barricading.

2. **Stay Low:** Crouch while moving items to avoid being seen through windows. Be careful to manage your noise if moving objects to the door.

3. **Block Windows:** If the door has windows, cover them, if possible, to block the view inside.

Using Body Weight for Added Protection

If furniture is not available or not heavy enough, you may need to add body weight to the barricade. Here's how to do it:

1. **Lean against the Barricade:** Position yourself against the barricade, adding pressure from your body. Be mindful that bullets go through doors, and be careful of bullet penetration.
2. **Sit or Brace Your Back:** Sit with your back against heavy furniture, applying additional force.
3. **Rotate with Others:** If others are with you, take turns pressing against the barricade so everyone gets a break.

Tips for Barricading in Different Areas like Patient Rooms

In patient rooms, use the bed as a primary barricading tool:

1. **Roll the Bed:** Move the bed close to the door.
2. **Lock the Bed's Wheels:** Most hospital beds have wheel locks to keep them from moving.
3. **Add Chairs and Tables:** Use chairs and bedside tables to reinforce the barricade.

In offices and supply rooms:

1. **Use Desks and Cabinets:** Desks are great for barricading because they're heavy and often fit well against the door.
2. **Close Drawers:** Full drawers add more weight to cabinets and desks, making it harder to move.

When Traditional Options Aren't Available

If you're in a location with limited furniture, try these options:

1. **Towels and Fabric Rolls:** Tuck towels or fabric under the door to make it harder to open.
2. **Bathroom Fixtures:** In bathrooms, use trash cans, toilet paper dispensers, and other fixtures to create a barrier.

Homemade Door Wedges

A simple door wedge can be a lifesaver. You can create one by:

1. **Using a Block of Wood:** Cut or break a piece of wood to fit under the door.
2. **Kicking It in Place:** Slide it under the door with a firm kick to create a strong wedge.

Remember, make sure the wedge does not stick out on the other side where it can be noticed.

Barricading With Available Supplies

In a healthcare setting, you may have access to certain items that can help with barricading:

1. **Medical Tapes and Bandages:** Use these to secure small items or even the door handle.
2. **Electrical Cords:** Tie off cords around the door handle and anchor them to heavy objects.

Staying Calm While Barricading

Remember to remain calm during this process is crucial:

1. **Autogenic Breathing:** Take deep breaths to stay centered and focused. Remember your "Showtime."

2. **Work as a Team:** Communicate with others in the room, assign tasks, and work together.

3. **Remember the goal:** Each step of the barricade is meant to buy time and protect yourself.

After the Barricade is in place, you'll need to stay quiet and wait for help:

1. **Follow your protocol** for confirming the identity of your law enforcement with such tactics as using an agreed password or sliding a green card under the door. Be mindful that if a staff member is a threat, they may know your password or have a safety card.

2. **Listen for Signs of Safety:** Stay alert to any instructions over the intercom or from emergency responders.

3. ***Do Not Make Noise:*** *Avoid moving or talking loudly, as this can draw attention. Many people strongly tend not to realize how loudly they speak while on the phone, even when they think they are being quiet.*

Discreet Communication:

Additionally, introduces the concept of "night whispering," a technique for discreet communication during high-stress situations. This involves softly speaking directly into someone's ear while exhaling first to minimize sound and avoid detection. Emphasize the importance of this method for maintaining privacy and safety in critical moments.

4. **Have an Exit Strategy:** Even if barricaded, you should know how to get out if the barricade fails.

Final Thoughts on Barricading

In a healthcare environment, barricading can save lives. By using the items around you, positioning yourself strategically, and staying calm, you can create a safer space when escape isn't possible.

Sometimes, you may have to give the visual impression that you are not in the room. Lower the lights rather than turning them off. Partially close the door if you are unable to lock it.

Chapter 12

Defending yourself and others When You Can't Escape

Defending yourself is the LAST RESORT. If escape is not possible and you have already barricaded yourself from danger, then you are the last line of defense until rescuers arrive.

When facing danger, it's important to know your options. If you can't escape or barricade yourself from the attacker, the last choice is to defend yourself. Defending means taking action to stay safe and protecting those around you. Here's how to do it with confidence and clear thinking.

One of my favorite quotes on this is from Tony Sherman, President of Genesis Group, "Your inability to take action will produce ineffective results."

When the decision is made to defend your life, you need to be all in. All in means emotionally invested, mentally alert, and physically ready to do what it takes to stay alive.

A phrase often associated with Vietnam War veterans captures this mindset well:

"You learn that life is about survival and doing whatever it takes to stay alive. Out there, it's you, your brothers, and the will to make it through." At the same time, it appeared in various forms across different interviews, books, and media. It reflects a sentiment shared by many veterans about the harsh realities of survival in combat.

Another well-known phrase from that era, reflecting the gritty determination to survive, is: "There are no heroes out here. Just survivors."

A true survivor will overcome their fear and inhibitions to accomplish the task at hand. There is a survivor in all of us. This is the survival mindset!

The Right to Self-Defense in Healthcare Settings

The right to defend oneself in a healthcare setting is a nuanced application of self-defense principles, as healthcare environments are often high-stress, high-risk places where employees, patients, and visitors may face potential threats from aggressive or violent individuals. The reason many fail at making this decision is they focus on the results of failing and not the steps to survive.

Here's how self-defense typically applies in these settings:

1. Reasonable Belief and Proportional Force

Healthcare workers have the right to defend themselves when they have a reasonable belief that they are in imminent danger of harm. However, their response must align with the principle of proportional force, consistent with general self-defense laws. [37] This means that the

[37] (National Institute for Occupational Safety and Health [NIOSH], 2021).

level of force used should not exceed what is necessary to address the threat.

For instance, when faced with non-lethal threats, healthcare workers are often encouraged or legally advised to use non-lethal techniques such as:

- Non-escalation and de-escalation strategies.
- Escaping measures.
- Barricading the situation rather than resorting to physical force.
- Defending as a last resort option.

Additionally, OSHA is preparing to release a proposed standard on workplace violence prevention in healthcare settings in December 2024. These approaches help minimize harm while ensuring the safety of both the worker and the patient. [38]

2. Duty to Retreat and Workplace Safety Policies

Some states prioritize the "duty to retreat," encouraging citizens to avoid or escape potentially dangerous situations rather than confront them. Programs that follow the Run, Hide, Fight doctrine parallel to this. In addition, this duty may differ in the home verses out of the home. It is important to understand the legal distinction in the area that we are in. Please refer to the Castle Doctrine for your state.

---

[38] (OSHA Slated to Deliver Proposed Workplace Violence Prevention Standard for Healthcare Industry in December 2024, 2024)

3. Limited Use of Force in Healthcare Active Shooter Incidents

Many healthcare facilities impose strict limitations on the use of physical force, particularly in active shooter situations, due to regulatory requirements and patient care standards with the priority is to ensure patient and staff safety while adhering to legal and ethical obligations.

Most healthcare institutions emphasize non-physical interventions, including crisis intervention and conflict resolution training, to equip staff with de-escalation strategies whenever possible. [39]

However, during an active shooter event, staff are encouraged to follow Run, Hide, and Fight protocols, prioritizing evacuation and securing patients in safe areas before resorting to force as a last resort. [40]

These restrictions aim to minimize harm, particularly to patients who may be vulnerable, physically incapacitated, or experiencing mental health crises. Healthcare workers must balance personal safety, duty to care, and legal constraints in responding to violent threats.[41]

Legal Protections and Workplace policies

- **Self-Defense Laws:** In many jurisdictions, individuals, including healthcare workers, have the right to defend themselves if they reasonably believe they are in imminent

[39] (U.S. Department of Health & Human Services [HHS], 2022).
[40] (Federal Emergency Management Agency [FEMA], 2021).
[41] (OSHA, 2012).

danger. This right is typically contingent upon the use of force being proportionate to the threat faced.

- **OSHA Guidelines on Workplace Violence Prevention:** The Occupational Safety and Health Administration (OSHA) acknowledges the prevalence of workplace violence in healthcare settings. It emphasizes the importance of training healthcare workers in de-escalation techniques and appropriate responses to threats. OSHA's Guidelines for Preventing Workplace Violence for Healthcare and Social Service Workers provide comprehensive recommendations for developing policies and procedures to mitigate workplace violence.
- **Proportional Use of Force:** While OSHA does not explicitly detail self-defense laws, it recognizes the need for healthcare workers to be prepared to handle situations where they may face imminent danger.

The guidelines suggest that training programs should include information on the appropriate use of force and emphasize that any physical interventions must be proportionate to the threat faced. This approach aligns with general self-defense principles, which permit individuals to protect themselves when they reasonably believe they are in imminent danger, provided their response is proportionate.

- **Understanding Facility Policies and Legal Standards:** It is important for healthcare workers to be familiar with both their facility's policies and the legal standards governing self-defense in their jurisdiction. Regular training and a clear understanding of acceptable interventions can help mitigate potential liabilities. [42]

- **Workplace Policies:** Healthcare facilities often have specific policies regarding the use of force. Adherence to these policies is crucial, as deviation can lead to disciplinary actions or liability. For instance, the Occupational Safety and Health Administration (OSHA) emphasizes the importance of training healthcare workers in de-escalation techniques and the appropriate use of force. [43]

Potential Liabilities:

- **Excessive Force:** Using force that exceeds what is deemed reasonable under the circumstances can result in legal consequences, including criminal charges or civil lawsuits.
- **Unapproved Methods:** Employing techniques or interventions not sanctioned by the facility can lead to liability, especially if they result in harm.

Key Considerations for Justifiable Self-Defense in Healthcare:

Unapproved Methods: Employing techniques or interventions not sanctioned by the facility can lead to liability, especially if they result in harm.

[42] (Prevention of Workplace Violence in Healthcare and Social Assistance | Occupational Safety and Health Administration, n.d.)

[43] (Healthcare - Workplace Violence | OSHA.gov | Occupational Safety and Health Administration, 2016)

There are three types of justifiable responses:

1 **Trained Techniques:** These are clear applications of the classroom model. Healthcare workers trained in specific self-defense or restraint techniques should adhere to their training. Proper application of these techniques, as taught, performed when appropriate, generally legal protection.

2 **Dynamic Application of Trained Techniques:** Situations can evolve rapidly, requiring workers to adapt their responses. These are not the exact classroom models, but they are as close as possible under the circumstances. These actions taken in good faith to prevent harm are often legally defensible, provided they are reasonable and proportionate.

3 **Not trained but Justifiable Actions:** When a worker has not received specific training, actions taken to defend oneself or others can still be justified. The key determinants are the reasonableness of the belief of imminent harm and the proportionality of the response.

It's essential for healthcare workers to be familiar with both their facility's policies and the legal standards governing self-defense in their jurisdiction. Regular training and a clear understanding of acceptable interventions can help mitigate potential liabilities.

Assistance from Security and Law Enforcement

In situations where a serious threat exists, healthcare facilities often rely on in-house security teams or law enforcement rather than expecting untrained staff to handle the threat alone. Some facilities also employ safety alert systems and other protocols to summon security quickly in case of an emergency.

In healthcare settings, safety and liability concerns place unique constraints on self-defense. Following the facility's safety policies and legal guidelines for handling confrontations is essential.

The Right to Defend Self and Others during an Active Assailant Incident

In an active assailant incident, individuals may need to defend themselves and others as a last resort when escape or barricading is impossible. The right to self-defense is widely recognized under law and allows individuals to use reasonable force to protect themselves or others from imminent harm.

Legal Framework

1. Defense of others in many legal systems extends the right of self-defense, including protecting others in imminent danger. Known as the "defense of others" doctrine, individuals can intervene if they reasonably believe someone is at risk of harm.

2. In some jurisdictions, the duty to "Retreat vs. Stand Your Ground" imposes a duty to retreat if it is safe before using force. In contrast, others adopt "stand your ground" laws, which allow individuals to defend themselves without retreating if they are lawfully present.

Application in Healthcare and Workplace Settings

In a healthcare or workplace setting, the right to self-defense and defense of others may be invoked when:

1. Staff and patients are under direct attack.
2. Immediate actions are necessary to prevent further harm.

Policies often encourage employees to prioritize de-escalation and evacuation. However, defending oneself or others becomes necessary and justified if confronted with an imminent threat.

Practical Guidelines for Defense in Healthcare Settings

Healthcare workers must be equipped with the knowledge and skills necessary to respond effectively and safely to an imminent threat, such as an active shooter or physical assault. Adhering to principles of proportionality, neutralization, and teamwork can significantly increase the chances of successfully defending oneself and others while minimizing harm. Below are more detailed practical guidelines to follow when faced with such a threat:

1. **Know the Limits of Force**

   - **Proportionality of Force:** Healthcare workers must ensure that any physical force used is proportional to the threat. This means responding with a level of force that is necessary to neutralize the threat without escalating it. For example, responding to a verbal threat may require verbal de-escalation techniques, whereas physical aggression may necessitate defensive actions to stop an immediate assault.

Excessive force, especially in the absence of a significant threat, can lead to legal liability or disciplinary action. [44]

- **Legal Protections:** Healthcare workers are often protected under self-defense laws when they act in good faith to prevent imminent harm to themselves or others. However, actions must remain within the bounds of reasonable force. Unnecessary or excessive force beyond what is needed to stop the threat could lead to criminal charges, civil lawsuits, or professional disciplinary actions. It's crucial to understand the facility's policies on acceptable force and to adhere to them in any emergency situation. (National Institute for Occupational Safety and Health).[45]

2 **Focus on Neutralizing the Threat**

- **Primary Objective:** When responding to a violent threat, the goal should always be to neutralize the threat to protect yourself, patients, and others. This means focusing on actions that will disarm or incapacitate the assailant, halting the attack effectively. In the context of healthcare, this involves stopping the aggressor from inflicting harm without escalating the situation unnecessarily.

- **Techniques for Neutralization:** If physically trained, healthcare workers may use restraint techniques, or self-defense moves to subdue or incapacitate an assailant. The

---

[44] (Occupational Safety and Health Administration)
[45] (CDC, 2024)

focus should always be on protecting lives, including the attackers, and minimizing harm to everyone involved. For example, trained professionals might use joint locks or pressure points as part of the effort to incapacitate without causing lasting harm (National Institute for Occupational Safety and Health).[46]

- **Escape and Evacuation:** If possible, the best course of action is often to evacuate the area and secure patients in a safe location while law enforcement handles the situation. Neutralization does not always require physical intervention; if feasible, relocating to a safe area and waiting for authorities may be the safest option for everyone involved.

3. Work as a Team

- **Coordinate with Others**: In an active threat situation, coordination among healthcare workers and security personnel is essential. When possible, establish a team-based response to neutralize the threat. Teamwork can involve directing colleagues to evacuate patients, securing exits, and alerting law enforcement. Coordination with other healthcare workers can also enhance the ability to control the situation safely and effectively.

- **Active Shooter Drills and Training**: Healthcare facilities should regularly conduct active shooter drills and training

[46] (NIOSH, 2021)

exercises that emphasize teamwork, role delegation, and communication. Having a predefined team response, including clear instructions for how to handle various situations, can save critical time in an emergency and ensure a unified approach.[47]

- **Effective Communication:** Effective communication during an emergency is crucial. Staff should be trained in using radios or other communication tools to relay information to security or law enforcement, as well as to communicate with each other during an active threat scenario.[48]

Summary:

By following these practical guidelines, healthcare workers can increase their safety and improve their ability to protect themselves and others during an active threat. Understanding the limits of force, focusing on neutralizing the threat, and working as a team are essential elements of a comprehensive defense strategy that respects legal boundaries and prioritizes patient care. Regular training, clear policies, and adherence to these principles are necessary to ensure that healthcare workers are prepared for violent situations and can act in a legally sound manner while safeguarding everyone's well-being.

The right to defend oneself and others is a critical safeguard during an active assailant incident, allowing individuals to act decisively when

[47] (Occupational Safety and Health Administration [OSHA], 2012).
[48] (Osha, 2012)

no other options remain. In active threat situations, healthcare workers must be prepared to defend themselves, even if security personnel or law enforcement (LE) are on their way. While security response times generally range around two minutes, law enforcement may take 7 to 12 minutes to arrive, depending on the location and community response time. [49] This delay, often referred to as the "response gap," highlights the need for a well-developed plan to protect oneself and others until help arrives.

Studies indicate that during an active attack, someone is injured or killed about every 15 seconds, reinforcing the urgency of immediate action. Furthermore, not all security personnel are armed or trained to confront a direct threat. In many cases, security personnel are trained to isolate the situation and help with evacuation rather than engage with the attacker. Therefore, healthcare workers must be equipped with the knowledge and skills to respond immediately and appropriately to an active threat, even in the absence of armed, trained security. [50]

Why We Defend Ourselves

Defending ourselves is a natural instinct. Untrained staff panic and fail, while trained staff are more focused and survive. Everyone deserves to feel safe. When faced with danger, people react in different ways. Some people freeze up, unsure of what to do, so they do nothing. Some flee, running without direction or focus. Some "freak out" with a combination of every reaction imaginable. Others fight and take the best

[49] (Cutting Your Team's Response Time in Half | Critical Arc, 2018)
[50] (Search Results | CDC, 2023)

action because they know what to expect. It's normal to feel scared but having a pre-planned and practiced plan helps us act with confidence.

Here's what to remember if you find yourself needing to defend yourself:

- Have a pre-planned practice response in mind - before the incident occurs
- Take action, be confident, and don't freeze
- When we prepare ahead of time, we're more likely to take focused, quick action.
- Trained and prepared people have a high level of survivability in dangerous situations.

Trust Your Instincts:

Your body will help you by overcoming the "freeze, flight, fight or freakout" response. Planning helps you control this reaction and make the best choices in critical moments.

Logical vs. Tactical Thinking: Stay Calm and Make Smart Decisions

In high-pressure situations, we rely on two main types of thinking: logical thinking and tactical thinking.

Logical Thinking: This is when you act quickly based on what's right in front of you. For example, if there's a small fire, you might grab the first cup of water to throw on it because water usually puts out fires.

Tactical Thinking: This is about looking at all your options and planning the best choice. Instead of grabbing the cup of water right away, a tactical thinker might look around and see if there's something else nearby that would work better, like a pot of dirt or carpet. Dirt can cover the fire better and stop it from spreading, and carpet may reduce oxygen, slowing down the fire's ability to spread.

How to Defend Yourself

If you're in a situation where you need to defend yourself and are unable to escape, follow these steps to stay as safe as possible:

- **Stay Focused if a Weapon Is Pointed at You**: Remain calm and use a steady voice. If you know the attacker's name, say it to get their attention and create a personal connection.

- **Humanize the Interaction:** Share your name to establish a sense of personal identity and potentially de-escalate the situation.

- **Prepare to Defend Yourself:** If the attacker moves too close, use strong, deliberate movements to push them away. Stay balanced and be ready to react quickly.

- **Use Nearby Objects as Tools for Defense:** Look around for everyday items that can serve as "weapons of opportunity" or distractions to help you create an opening for escape or defense.

An important Decision

Protecting your life is never an easy decision, especially when it means making the difficult choice to hurt someone or stop them from causing harm. In situations where your safety or the safety of others is at risk, you may be forced to act in self-defense, even if it involves confronting the threat directly. The instinct to protect oneself is powerful, but the act of defending yourself can bring feelings of guilt or moral conflict. However, the reality is that in moments of extreme danger, the primary concern must be survival. While it's not something anyone ever wants to do, sometimes stopping an attacker from hurting or killing you is the only way to preserve your own life and ensure the safety of those around you.

"Weapons of Opportunity" in Hospitals

In emergencies, ordinary items found in a hospital can become tools for self-defense. These weapons of opportunity do not require specialized training or tools, just creativity and quick thinking. Here are some examples:

1. **Sharp Objects:** Items such as pens, scissors, keys, or even medical instruments like syringes can be used to cut, stab, jab, or poke in defense. The side rails take a lot of effort; a safety pin from a fire extinguisher or fragments of broken glass can also serve as improvised sharp tools. Anything that you can use to inflict harm in an emergency may serve as a defensive tool.
2. **Heavy Items:** Use objects like medical trays, clipboards, IV poles, or even a fire extinguisher. A fire extinguisher can be

particularly versatile; spray it to disorient the attacker, create distance, obscure their vision, or use its weight to push them back.

By recognizing the potential of common hospital items, you can increase your ability to defend yourself and others in a dangerous situation.

Choosing the Right Object

Think about what's easy to grab, what won't hurt you to use, and what gives you some distance from the attacker. Heavy objects might give you more power, but smaller, sharp items are easier to handle and move.

In choosing an appropriate object, there are three criteria to consider:

1. How much distance do you have from the threat?
2. How much physical effort will you have to use for this item to be effective?
3. What is your desired outcome?

Considerations for Fire Extinguishers.

A fire extinguisher can be an effective defensive tool, but using it requires physical strength, commitment, and strategic thinking.

1. **Using as a Blunt-Force Weapon:** If you are alone, wielding a fire extinguisher for defense requires both hands and a significant amount of physical energy. Striking an attacker over

the head is a high-commitment action. Keep in mind that an armed attacker may have a firearm, making it crucial to act decisively and with precision.

2. If possible, remove the safety pin from the fire extinguisher. The pin itself can serve as a puncturing tool in self-defense. Additionally, with one hand, you can control the attacker's weapon while using a weapon of choice in the other.

If You Become a Hostage

At the time of this publishing, there were no documented cases of hostages being taken during an active shooter incident. [51]If you are the most important goal is to survive. Here's what to do:[52]

1. **Stay Calm and be cooperative:** Don't argue and avoid making sudden movements. Follow any instructions without resistance.
2. **Observe Details:** Notice anything about the attacker, like their clothing, speech, or any unique features (like scars or tattoos). This could be helpful later.
3. **Identify Scent or Odor:** Noting unusual smells (such as cigarettes, cologne, or body odor) may later help in identifying the individual.
4. **Stay Low During a Rescue:** If law enforcement or rescuers come, stay calm and keep your hands visible with palms facing

---

[51] (Redirecting, 2025)
[52] (Young, 2018)

upward. If possible, stay low or find cover to avoid being mistaken for a threat.

What to Remember in a Dangerous Situation

1. **Plan and Practice:** Just like you practice fire drills, it's important to think ahead about what you would do in an emergency.
2. **Use Tactical Thinking:** Apply critical thinking for immediate survivability and escape. Assess your options carefully and choose the one that maximizes your safety.
3. **Be Ready to Act:** If you cannot escape or block the attacker, use the tools and training you have to defend yourself.
4. **Stay Observant and Calm:** Keeping a clear mind helps you make smart choices and stay safe. Where is the threat and my exits is there a clear path?
5. **Use Your Surroundings:** Look around to see what objects might be helpful for defense if needed.

Remember, even though these situations are rare, being prepared can make all the difference. Knowing what to do can help keep you and others safe. Once you decide to defend yourself, let's talk about the setup and positioning.

Setup and Positioning for Defense

Setup: Choosing the Best Position

The most strategic location to stop an attacker is at the doorway. The farther they move into a room, the lower your chances of staying safe.

There are two central setup positions:

- **The "Long Side" (Hinge Side):** This is where the door's hinges are located. You will have to move farther to reach the attacker, making this a less effective position for contact.
- **The "Short Side" (Opening Side)**: This is where the door swings into the room. It is the best setup position for defense. By trapping the attacker in the doorway, you limit their movement and control their ability to raise, lower, or swing their weapon. This also forces them to step backwards, away from the room.

Position: The Advantage of Staying Low

When you are on the short side of the door, your best position is to crouch below the doorknob.

Why Stay Low?

In highly stressful situations, everyone gets what is referred to as tunnel vision. In this condition, a person's field of vision narrows, making it difficult to see anything outside of a minor, focused area straight ahead. This often happens in high-stress or dangerous situations when adrenaline is high, causing the brain to focus intensely on one threat or task and ignore everything else around it.

In survival situations, tunnel vision can help people concentrate on immediate danger. Still, it can also be risky because it reduces awareness of other important details or threats in the surroundings.

Positioning yourself lower than the doorknob keeps you out of the attacker's line of sight (their "tunnel vision") and gives you an advantage.

If you are alone and have no other weapons:

1. Get into a crouched position lower than the doorknob with both hands open and in front of you.
2. Do not cover or block the weapon's muzzle (barrel) to prevent being shot if it goes off.
3. Grab the weapon's center firmly as soon as it appears, extending your arms forward to push the muzzle high into the door frame/jamb as you disarm the threat.

Special Considerations for Disarming Handguns:

Please note the weapon operation in this text is for reference only and is offered in classes that are more focused and supervised training.

1. **Handgun:** Using both hands, grab the handgun's center, covering the trigger well. Rotate the muzzle toward the attacker's face. Keep rotating forward until they release their grip. Keeping the muzzle of the weapons pointed at the threat

2. Pull it into your control and create distance as you step offline, staying inside the room using the doorway as cover.

3. You may have to prepare the weapon in case you have to use it to save your life.

Types of Rifles and Long Guns

Various rifles and shotguns are designed for specific uses based on their action mechanisms and functionality. Bolt-action rifles, such as the Remington Model 700 and Winchester Model 70, require the shooter to manually operate a bolt to load and eject rounds, making them ideal for precision shooting and hunting. Lever-action rifles, like the Henry Lever Action and Winchester 1894, use a lever mechanism to chamber rounds and are often associated with classic cowboy firearms. Semi-automatic rifles, such as the AR-15 and Ruger 10/22, utilize energy from a fired round to cycle the action, allowing for one shot per trigger pull. Automatic rifles, including the M16 and automatic variants of the AK-47, can continuously fire as long as the trigger is held down and are primarily used by military forces. Pump-action rifles, like the Remington Model 7600, require manual operation of a sliding forearm to eject and chamber rounds. Break-action rifles, such as the Thompson/Center Contender, open at the breech for loading and are typically single-shot or multi-barrel. Single-shot rifles, like the Sharps Rifle and Ruger No. 1, require manual reloading after each shot and are prevalent in competitive shooting and hunting.

Additionally, bolt-action shotguns, such as the Mossberg 185, offer the power of a shotgun with a manually cycled action. Carbines, like the

M4 Carbine, are shorter rifles designed for better maneuverability in confined spaces. Shotguns, designed to fire multiple projectiles (shot) or slugs, come in different action types, including pump-action (Remington 870, Mossberg 500), semi-automatic (Benelli M4), and break-action (Browning Citori). Each firearm type has a unique purpose, from sport shooting and hunting to home defense and military use.

Each rifle or long gun type is suited to specific purposes, such as hunting, sport shooting, military use, or home defense, offering varying levels of precision, power, and handling.

Special considerations for disarming long guns:

Using both hands, grab the extended portion of the rifle, ensuring your hands does not block the muzzle. Use the hand closest to the stock to pull it toward you. Rotate the muzzle toward the attacker's face and keep rotating forward until they let go. Keep the muzzle of the weapons pointed at the threat.

1. Using both hands, grab the rifle's center, with one hand below the muzzle and the other at top of the stock. Rotate the muzzle upwards and into the attacker's face. Use the hand on the stock to pull it towards their body.

2. Rotate the rifle with the muzzle facing the attack until it releases its grip. Keep the muzzle of the weapons pointed at the threat

3. Pull it into your control and create distance as you step offline, staying inside the room using the doorway as cover.

4. You may have to prepare the weapon in case you have to use it to save your life.

    - Keep your finger off the trigger; you will tap the magazine if they use a semi-automatic.
    - Pull the slide back and release it to the forward position.
    - Breathe and evaluate the situation if further action is needed.

If you are alone and using complex objects or sharp instruments to aid you in disarming:

1. Remember, using a hard object will need maximum effort, and you will still need to control the weapon's muzzle.

If you have disarmed the threat, here are a few considerations to surrender the weapon to police when you meet them:

1. Never confront police with any weapons or items in your hands.
2. Place the weapon on the ground with the muzzle facing away from them
3. Place your hands above your head, palms open.
4. Follow instructions entirely without hesitation.

In an active shooter situation, healthcare workers must understand the risks involved, including the possibility of being mistakenly identified as a threat by law enforcement responders. When officers arrive on the scene, their primary objective is to neutralize the shooter and secure the area, often in a high-stress and rapidly evolving environment. This means that despite their best efforts to provide care and protect patients, healthcare workers may face situations where they or others are inadvertently perceived as a threat. It is essential to remain calm, follow all law enforcement instructions, keep hands visible, and avoid sudden movements to reduce this risk. By being aware of these realities and preparing accordingly, healthcare workers can improve their chances of staying safe while prioritizing patient care in a crisis.

Here are situations where innocent people can get accidentally shot during an active shooter incident:

1. **Police Misidentification of a Good Samaritan:** In some active shooter incidents, an innocent person attempting to stop the shooter has been mistaken for the assailant. For example, in active shooter situations, law enforcement officers may, in the chaos of the moment, mistakenly identify a Good Samaritan as the assailant, leading to tragic outcomes. A notable example occurred on June 21, 2021, in Arvada, Colorado, when Johnny Hurley, a civilian, confronted and fatally shot an active shooter, Ronald Troyke, who had earlier killed Officer Gordon Beesley. After neutralizing the threat, Hurley was fatally shot by an Arvada police officer who mistook him for the assailant. The officer, Kraig Brownlow, was later cleared of criminal charges, with prosecutors stating that his actions were legally justified. This incident underscores law enforcement's complexities and challenges during active shooter responses, where rapid decision-making is crucial. The misidentification of a Good

Samaritan highlights the need for continuous training and clear communication protocols to minimize such tragic outcomes. [53]

2. **Confusion During an Evacuation:** In an active shooter situation, crowded areas and panic can lead to accidental shootings. For example, in some instances, law enforcement or security personnel have accidentally shot fleeing individuals, mistaking their fast movement or suspicious behavior for an immediate threat, especially when bystanders move unpredictably or fail to comply quickly with officers' commands.

3. **Crossfire in Close Quarters:** In confined spaces like schools, offices, or hospitals, law enforcement engaging an active shooter can sometimes lead to crossfire situations where innocent people are inadvertently struck. This can happen if civilians are hiding nearby or attempting to flee, resulting in accidental injuries or fatalities when caught in the line of fire.

These situations highlight the complexities and risks involved in active shooter responses, emphasizing the need for clear communication, identification protocols, and situational awareness among responders and civilians alike.

[53] (Mark, 2022)

Chapter 13

Providing Immediate, Self, and First Aid to Others

Please remember that this book is intended for ALL people working in a healthcare facility, whether or not they have any medical training. This section is designed to provide basic 1st and self-aid information for anyone needing it.

Providing Immediate Aid in an Active Assailant Incident

In emergencies, healthcare staff are often required to provide immediate first aid to stabilize injuries until further help arrives. In the case of an active assailant incident, knowing how to perform essential first aid tasks like stopping bleeding or managing shock can be lifesaving for patients, colleagues, or even oneself.

During active assailant incidents, you may have to aid yourself, others, or even the assailant themselves. This chapter provides a comprehensive guide on administering basic first aid during critical incidents, particularly in healthcare environments. Providing Immediate Aid, Self-Aid and First Aid to others.

The Importance of Immediate First Aid

First aid is the initial care given to someone experiencing an injury or sudden illness. In high-stress, life-threatening situations, like an active assailant incident, quick, skilled first aid can be the difference between life and death. Healthcare staff are trained in various medical procedures, but immediate actions take precedence in these scenarios. Prompt intervention to control bleeding, protect airways and manage shock is crucial, as every second counts.

Basic Principles of Emergency First Aid

1. **Assess the Situation**: Before intervening, quickly assess the surroundings for immediate dangers to yourself or others. Ensuring your safety is paramount, as you cannot assist others if incapacitated.

2. **Prioritize Life-Threatening Injuries:** In emergencies, prioritize injuries that are immediately life-threatening, such as severe bleeding, obstructed airways, and shock. Start with the most critical issues and work down as you stabilize the individual.

3. **Stay Calm and Provide Reassurance:** Calmly and confidently communicate with the injured person. Reassuring patients, colleagues, or bystanders helps alleviate panic and improve cooperation during life-saving procedures. You may also request any assistance from bystanders to help with care, e.g., to apply direct pressure to life-threatening bleeding while you assess and treat other life threats.

Essential First Aid Techniques for Healthcare Emergencies: Managing Bleeding, Airway and Shock

1. **Stopping Severe Life-Threatening Bleeding**

   a. **Apply Direct Pressure:** Place a clean, absorbent cloth or gauze pad over the wound and apply firm, direct pressure to stop or slow the bleeding. If the cloth becomes soaked with blood, add more layers rather than removing the soaked material to maintain pressure. Even using your body weight if nothing else is available. If the wounded individual is conscious and capable, they may provide direct pressure on their wound, thereby freeing you up to continue assessing/treating life-threatening injuries.

   b. **Use a Tourniquet:** If bleeding from an arm or leg cannot be controlled with direct pressure, apply a tourniquet. Position it above the wound and tighten it until the bleeding stops. Mark the time on the tourniquet for medical personnel to assess the duration it has been applied for. While a commercial tourniquet is preferred, this may need to be a cord or wire. Typically, an IV tourniquet will not provide sufficient pressure to stop an arterial bleeding.

   c. **Pack the Wound:** Use clean gauze or hemostatic dressing to pack the wound cavity for deep, severe wounds. Push the material into the wound as deeply as possible and apply continuous pressure to control the bleeding. This may be using small parts of the patient's or your clothing.

2. **Maintaining Airway and Breathing:**

   a. **Check for Obstruction:** If the individual is not breathing or struggling to breathe, inspect the mouth and throat for any visible obstructions. If you see an object blocking the airway, carefully remove it using a sweeping motion, but only if it is safe.

   b. **Positioning:** If the person is unconscious but breathing, tilt the head slightly back to open the airway. However, if a spinal injury is suspected, use the jaw-thrust technique instead of tilting the head to avoid further neck injury.

   c. **Recovery Position:** If the individual is breathing, unconscious, and has no life-threatening bleeding, place them in the recovery position to prevent airway obstruction. This helps keep the airway clear and reduces the risk of choking.

3. Recognize Symptoms of Shock:

In an emergency, symptoms of shock include pale or clammy skin, rapid pulse, shallow breathing, confusion, or unconsciousness. Shock is often a result of significant blood loss or severe injury and needs immediate attention.

   a. **Keep Them Warm and Calm:** Use blankets or clothing to keep the person warm, as hypothermia can worsen shock. Speak reassuringly and avoid giving them food or drink, which could lead to choking.

b. **Lay the person flat:** Position the individual on their back to help maintain blood flow to vital organs. Elevate the legs slightly if no spinal injury is suspected.

4. **Using Basic First Aid Equipment in Healthcare Settings**

a. **Tourniquets:** Familiarize yourself with different types of tourniquets available in healthcare and practice applying them correctly. Tourniquets are critical tools for controlling limb hemorrhages.

b. **Hemostatic Dressings:** These specialized dressings promote clotting and are essential for deep wounds with excessive bleeding.

c. **Pressure Bandages:** These are particularly useful for injuries in locations where a tourniquet cannot be applied, such as the abdomen or head. Apply a pressure bandage by wrapping it snugly around the wound and adding additional padding to help control bleeding.

d. **CPR (Cardiopulmonary Resuscitation):** If the person is unresponsive and not breathing, begin CPR immediately. Provide chest compressions at a rate of 100-120 compressions per minute, pressing down firmly and evenly in the center of the chest.

e. **AEDs (Automated External Defibrillators):** AEDs are essential for cardiac emergencies. Be familiar with the location and operation of AED units in your healthcare facility. Using an AED in the first minutes of a cardiac event can significantly improve survival rates.

5. **Providing Care Under Stressful Conditions**

    a. **Building Preparedness Through Regular Practice:** Maintaining a clear head and methodical approach during high-stress events can save lives. Healthcare providers should practice these skills regularly to build muscle memory, making responses more effective and swifter during emergencies.

    b. **Practice Breathing and Focus Techniques:** During an emergency, you may need to remind yourself to take deep, calming breaths. Practicing breathing techniques during training can improve focus and reduce panic.

    c. **Work as a Team:** In a healthcare setting, teamwork is crucial. Clear communication and designated roles can make first aid more effective. Assign tasks (like applying pressure or fetching equipment) to different team members to streamline care.

6. **Addressing Special Situations in Healthcare Settings**

    a. **Chemical Injuries:** If a patient or staff member sustains a chemical burn, rinse the affected area with large amounts of clean water and avoid touching the substance. For eye exposure, use an eyewash station if available.

b. **Fractures and Immobilization:** If you suspect a fracture, stabilize the injured area with a splint. Avoid moving the individual if you suspect a spinal injury, as this could lead to further harm.

c. **Burns:** Cool the area with water and cover it with a clean, non-stick cloth for thermal burns. Avoid applying ointments or lotions to severe burns.

7. **Psychological First Aid (PFA) for Patients and Staff**

   a. **Psychological First Aid:** It is as important as physical first aid, especially in a traumatic event like an active assailant incident. PFA helps reduce stress and provides emotional support.

   b. **Listen Actively:** Allow individuals to express their feelings, providing a calm, non-judgmental ear. Many people experience intense emotions, and listening can help them process the situation.

   c. **Provide Reassurance:** Validate their experiences and remind them that their reactions are typical in such circumstances.

   d. **Encourage Basic Self-Care:** Simple acts like drinking water, deep breathing, and taking breaks can help individuals cope with trauma.

8. Post-Emergency Considerations

a. **Post-Emergency Care and Documentation:** After the immediate danger has passed, healthcare staff should check for injuries and continue to monitor injured people. Ensuring accurate records will aid in continued care for the wounded and assist in future training and improvement of emergency response protocols.

b. **Debrief with Colleagues:** Conduct a post-incident debrief to review what went well and what could be improved. This helps prepare staff for future events and reinforces a supportive, cohesive environment.

c. **Seek Support if Needed:** Healthcare workers might need to support themselves in the aftermath of traumatic events. Peer support groups, mental health resources, and counseling can be valuable.

Final considerations

Providing first aid in healthcare settings during emergencies requires a unique blend of skill, calmness, and preparedness. By mastering basic first aid techniques such as controlling bleeding, maintaining clear airways, and managing shock, healthcare staff can make a crucial difference in survival rates. Regular training, practice, and familiarity with emergency equipment are essential to providing effective first aid during critical incidents.

Chapter 14

Mental Health Support After an Incident

After experiencing an active assailant situation, addressing mental health needs is critical. Healthcare staff, patients, and families may experience anxiety, stress, or trauma. Providing mental health support and understanding the resources available for post-incident care can aid recovery. This checklist serves as a guide to supporting mental health and well-being after a traumatic event, ensuring a path toward healing and resilience.

Why is Mental Health Support Essential After a Traumatic Incident

Experiencing a traumatic event can have lasting effects on individuals. It's common for people to feel scared, anxious, or overwhelmed. These feelings can affect work, daily life, and relationships. Mental health support helps those affected process their feelings and understand that these responses are normal. Support and resources can improve well-being and prevent long-term effects.

Key Components of a Mental Health Support Checklist

1. Initial Assessment and Immediate Support

a. Conduct immediate check-ins and follow the event; check in with staff, patients, and families as soon as it's safe. Ask if they are okay and listen to any concerns they might have. Acknowledging the event and showing empathy is essential in the initial stages.

b. Address immediate needs by providing those affected with physical comfort (like blankets, water, or a safe space). Physical demands are often overlooked but can help individuals feel secure and cared for.

c. Identify those needing immediate assistance and remember that some individuals may show more intense distress or may have had previous experiences with trauma. Ensure they receive immediate attention from a counselor or mental health professional.

2. Providing Emotional Support

Offer emotional and psychological first aid by listening actively and allowing individuals to talk about their feelings if they want to. Avoid giving advice or judgments. Just listening can be very therapeutic.

a. Reassure individuals that their reactions are expected in response to such a stressful event. Let them know that feeling anxious, sad, or even numb is part of the body's natural reaction to trauma.

b. Encourage essential self-care by suggesting simple steps like taking deep breaths, drinking water, and resting. Self-care is crucial in grounding the person and helping them regain control.

3. Establish peer support networks by creating a safe environment for sharing: Encourage team members or patients to share their feelings in a secure, non-judgmental environment. Peer support helps individuals feel less alone and validates their experiences.

   a. Form peer support groups if possible, and set up small groups where people can meet to discuss their feelings. Sometimes, knowing others have had similar reactions can reduce feelings of isolation.

   b. Assign peer leaders and designate trained peer leaders or mental health advocates within each group who can provide additional support and direct individuals to resources as needed.

4. Connecting to Mental Health Resources

Provide access to professional mental health services and connect with counseling resources. Make sure that everyone knows where and how to access counseling services. Provide contact details for counselors, therapists, and any available support hotlines.

a. Offer regular mental health check-ins and schedule follow-up sessions for counseling to ensure that individuals are coping well in the days and weeks after the incident.

b. Promote confidentiality and emphasize that mental health services are confidential. This helps reduce any stigma around seeking help.

5. Promoting Positive Coping Strategies

Encouraging positive coping strategies by teaching relaxation techniques that are simple techniques like deep breathing, meditation, and grounding exercises can be very helpful in reducing anxiety. Share guides or resources on these techniques with staff and patients.

a. Encouraging physical activities that are light exercises, such as walking or stretching, can help reduce stress and improve mood. Consider organizing group activities, if possible, like a walk or gentle stretching session.

b. Promoting healthy eating and sleeping habits by offering balanced diets and sound sleep is essential for mental health. Share tips on eating well and establishing a relaxing bedtime routine.

c. Implement long-term mental health follow-up with regular check-ins and schedule monthly or quarterly check-ins for affected staff and patients. Many people may feel okay initially but struggle later as they process the event.

d. Provide ongoing access to support services. Ensure that counseling and mental health resources remain available as long as needed. Recovery from trauma is different for everyone.

e. Consider post-traumatic stress disorder (PTSD) screening for individuals showing ongoing distress, consider screening for PTSD. Early intervention is key to managing the long-term effects of trauma.

6. **Building Mental Health Awareness and Resilience**

Provide educational resources and training on mental health and trauma issues. Distribute easy-to-understand information on common trauma responses and the benefits of mental health support. Offer Training Sessions: Host workshops on mental health awareness, self-care strategies, and stress management techniques. These sessions can help people recognize signs of trauma in themselves and others.

7. **Enhancing Mental Health Literacy**

Encouraging mental health literacy by teaching people to understand mental health terminology can empower them to seek support and understand their own experiences better.

8. **Supporting Families and Community Resources**

Family support and community resources for family members, and families of patients or staff may also need support. Please provide them with information on counseling services and community resources.

a. **Offer Group Counseling for Families:** If possible, arrange group counseling for family members. It can help them understand what their loved ones are going through and offer them a chance to express their concerns.

b. **Provide Access to Hotlines and Community Support:** Make information on helplines, community centers, and support groups available. Many people find community resources helpful during their recovery.

c. **Self-Care Checklist for Healthcare Staff:** Supporting others after a traumatic event can be mentally and emotionally draining. Healthcare staff need self-care to continue providing support effectively.

d. **Prioritize Rest:** Fatigue can make it harder to process stress. Encourage staff to take breaks and rest as needed.

e. **Seek Support for Yourself:** Remind staff that they should also reach out to peers, counselors, or support groups if they need to talk about their experiences.

f. **Practice Healthy Boundaries:** Helping others is essential; staff should be encouraged to maintain personal boundaries to protect their **well-being.**

g. **Engage in Personal Hobbies:** Whether reading, gardening, or other hobbies, doing activities they enjoy can help staff members unwind.

h. **Encourage Reflection and Journaling:** Writing down thoughts and feelings can be therapeutic. Provide journals or encourage reflection to help with processing emotions.

i. **Supporting Patients' Mental Health Needs:** Healthcare providers should also support patients who may experience long-term trauma after an incident. Encourage Open Communication: Patients should feel they can express their feelings about the incident without judgment. Checking in on their mental health periodically reinforces that their emotional recovery is important.

j. **Provide Safe Spaces:** Create areas within the facility where patients can relax or have private conversations with counselors. Be Patient and Understanding: Some patients may not initially want to discuss the event. Respect their pace and reassure them that support is available whenever needed.

Recovering from an active assailant incident takes time, compassion, and continuous support. By providing a structured mental health support checklist, healthcare facilities can create an environment that promotes healing for staff and patients. This checklist emphasizes empathy, proactive support, and consistent follow-up, ensuring everyone affected has the resources to process and recover from the trauma. With proper mental health support, individuals can gradually regain a sense of safety, stability, and resilience.

In the aftermath of an active shooter incident, hospitals can benefit from the support of various mental health organizations that specialize in trauma recovery and crisis intervention. Below is a list of such organizations:

1. American Psychological Association (APA) Offers resources and guidelines for trauma response and mental health support. [54]
2. National Mass Violence Victimization Resource Center (NMVVRC) Provides training and technical assistance for communities affected by mass violence. [55]
3. Substance Abuse and Mental Health Services Administration (SAMHSA) offers disaster behavioral health resources and crisis counseling assistance. [56]
4. The National Center for PTSD provides resources and research on trauma and PTSD, including treatment options.[57]
5. The International Critical Incident Stress Foundation (ICISF) offers training and support for critical incident stress management. [58]
6. The Joint Commission provides guidelines and resources for healthcare organizations to prepare for and respond to active shooter situations.[59]
7. Centers for Disease Control and Prevention [60]

[54] (APA, 2024)
[55] (National Mass Violence Center | NMVC, 2024)
[56] (Disaster Behavioral Health Resources, 2024)
[57] (Center, 2020)
[58] (ICISF, 2024)
[59] (Workforce Safety and Well-Being: Workplace Violence Prevention Program, 2025)
[60] (CDC) (Violence in Healthcare | Blogs | CDC, 2015)

8. Federal Emergency Management Agency (FEMA) provides crisis counseling assistance and training programs for disaster response.

9. The National Alliance on Mental Illness (NAMI) offers support and education for individuals affected by mental health conditions, including crisis intervention resources.[61]

10. The American Red Cross provides disaster mental health services and support for communities recovering from traumatic events.[62]

These organizations can provide resource materials and guidance to hospitals in developing and implementing effective mental health recovery plans following active shooter incidents.

---

61 (Navigating a Mental Health Crisis, 2024)

62 (Disaster Mental Health, 2020)

Chapter 15

Working with Hospital Security and Emergency Response Teams

In healthcare settings like hospitals, clinics, and outpatient facilities, active assailant situations require quick, coordinated responses to ensure the safety of patients, staff, and visitors. Healthcare staff must understand how to work effectively with their security teams and emergency responders during such events. This chapter provides guidelines on communicating and collaborating with security and emergency teams to enhance safety in critical moments.

Why Working with Security and Emergency Teams is Important

During an active assailant event, healthcare staff are often the first to identify potential threats and must quickly engage with security and emergency personnel. Effective communication and collaboration can mean a safe resolution and an escalated situation. By working closely with security and emergency teams, healthcare staff help create a coordinated response that maximizes the protection of everyone involved.

Understanding the Chain of Command in an Emergency

Understanding the chain of command is crucial for an effective response in an emergency. The chain of command defines who is responsible for making decisions and taking action during a crisis. In healthcare settings, security personnel or designated emergency management leaders typically take charge of the situation, coordinating with external emergency responders, such as law enforcement and fire departments.

Following the chain of command, everyone is clear on their roles, reducing confusion and preventing conflicting messages. This ensures that all efforts are focused on a unified goal: protecting the lives of patients, staff, and visitors.

Effective Communication in Emergencies

Clear communication with security and emergency teams is crucial. Healthcare staff should provide concise, accurate information to assist security teams in understanding the situation and planning a response. Avoid jargon or overly complex explanations and focus on the facts.

When communicating with emergency personnel, staff should remember the following:

1. Remain calm and speak SLOWLY and clearly. Speaking slowly will reduce the time you have to repeat information, saving time and lives!

2. Report essential information, such as the assailant's location, appearance, and any observed weapon.

a. Number of threats

b. Any names used

c. Accents, dialects

3. Follow security instructions promptly.

a. Ensure you are in a SAFE place when calling.

Effective communication allows emergency teams to act faster and more efficiently, minimizing risk to everyone involved.

Following Security Protocols

Healthcare facilities have established security protocols designed to protect staff, patients, and visitors in the event of an active assailant. These protocols may include escape, barricade procedures, or areas to wait-in-place orders.

During an active assailant event, healthcare staff must adhere to these protocols and follow instructions from security personnel without hesitation. Security protocols ensure consistent response and that emergency teams can rely on staff to uphold the facility's safety measures.

By adhering to these guidelines, healthcare staff can significantly reduce the risk of harm and help maintain order in a high-stress situation.

This book recommends all healthcare staff:

1. Stay informed about the facility's emergency response plan.

2. Participate in regular training and drills to be prepared for an active assailant scenario.

3. Communicate effectively with security teams and patients, offering reassurance without disclosing unnecessary details.

Supporting Emergency Responders & Advance Planning

External emergency responders, including armed healthcare security, police, SWAT teams, and paramedics, are trained to handle high-risk situations. Healthcare staff can assist by providing key information about the facility's layout, hazards, and patient locations. Joint training sessions can clarify response expectations for everyone involved.

By maintaining calm and offering helpful information, healthcare staff can help responders perform more effectively, improving overall safety. Additionally, providing a go-bag, outside access keys/cards, and conducting annual orientation walk-throughs can enhance preparedness and familiarity with the building.

Training and Preparation

Regular training and preparedness drills are essential for ensuring healthcare staff are ready to respond to an active assailant event. These drills should include simulations of real-life scenarios, emphasizing communication, quick decision-making, and collaboration with security and emergency teams.

Healthcare facilities should invest in regular training sessions that cover:

1. Emergency communication strategies.

2. Protocols for escaping, barricading, and defending.
3. Situational awareness and recognizing signs of potential threats.

Through training and preparation, healthcare staff become better equipped to handle emergencies, ultimately protecting patients, colleagues, and themselves.

In closing, in an active assailant situation, healthcare staff play a vital role in supporting security and emergency teams. By understanding the chain of command, communicating effectively, following security protocols, and participating in regular training, healthcare workers can help ensure a coordinated and effective response to keep everyone safe.

Remember, your actions and collaboration with security and emergency teams can make a significant difference in the outcome of an emergency. Be prepared, stay calm, and work together to protect lives.

Chapter 16

Conducting Exercises and Practicing Preparedness

Healthcare facilities, such as hospitals, clinics, and outpatient centers, are places where people expect to feel safe. However, like any public space, they are not immune to potential threats, including active assailant situations. To ensure the safety of patients, staff, and visitors, it is essential to conduct regular exercises. These practices help healthcare staff respond effectively in an emergency, building confidence and ensuring everyone knows what to do under pressure. This can begin with someone walking into your area to ask a question and escalate from there.

The Importance of Regular Practice

Regular exercises are crucial for reinforcing safety protocols. In high-stress situations, it can be easy to forget even well-practiced routines. Repeating exercises helps make the response actions almost second nature so that staff members can act quickly and confidently.

Practice Drills also provide an opportunity to identify areas where safety plans may need improvement. Each time a drill is conducted, healthcare staff can observe and evaluate their actions, ensuring that the most effective procedures are in place to protect everyone involved.

Types of Practice Drills and Scenarios

There are several types of Practice Drills and scenarios that healthcare facilities can use to prepare staff for an active assailant event. Each type of drill serves a different purpose and helps staff practice various aspects of emergency response.

Here are some common types of Practice Drills and scenarios:

1. **Escape Exercises**: These exercises help staff practice moving patients and visitors to safe locations outside the building. Staff learn the quickest and safest routes for evacuation.
2. **Movement exercises:** Both individually and in small groups, these exercises can simulate scenarios where one or more staff members are presumed injured.
3. **First aid exercises:** Emphasizing bleeding control techniques for self-care and assisting others in emergencies.
4. **Scenario-Based Exercise**: It ensures tailored training that reflects the uniqueness of each department's floor plans, equipment, and patient population.

For example, start with a general overview of background and tactics, followed by drills. Then, extend the training to specific departments and clinics for more focused application.

5. **Barricade Exercises:** In some cases, the safest option is to select and barricade parts of the facility to prevent an assailant from entering. Barricade exercises help staff practice securing doors and creating safe areas for patients and visitors.

6. **Communication Exercises:** Communication is vital during an emergency. These exercises allow staff to practice using emergency communication non-verbals, passwords, or devices, such as radios or public address systems, and to coordinate effectively with security and emergency teams.

By practicing different exercises, healthcare staff become more familiar with their roles and responsibilities in an emergency.

Simulating Real-Life Scenarios

Simulating real-life scenarios is an effective way to prepare healthcare staff for an active assailant event. These scenarios help staff understand what an emergency might feel like, helping them stay calm and make quick decisions. *"Be aware: Training scenarios may trigger past trauma responses."*

Simulations should be as realistic as possible, with actors or volunteers playing the roles of patients, visitors, and even the assailant. By experiencing a simulated event, staff can practice recognizing signs of potential threats, reacting to unexpected situations, and working together to keep everyone safe.

Realistic simulations build confidence and allow healthcare staff to see how their actions and decisions can positively impact an emergency.

Before starting any exercise, it is crucial to make the proper notifications and place the signs and staff to alert anyone passing by that the event is a training exercise. We recommend using bright-colored signs and letter sizes that are significant enough to see before standing before it.

Practicing Escape Routes and Barricade Procedures

One key part of preparing for an active assailant event is practicing escape routes and barricade procedures. Every healthcare facility has unique features, such as multiple floors, separate wings, or various entry and exit points. Knowing the facility's layout and the best escape routes can save precious time during an emergency.

Healthcare staff should practice using different escape routes and familiarize themselves with all possible exits. Barricade procedures should also be practiced so that staff know what room to select based on the safer place criteria and how to quickly secure doors and create barriers to protect themselves and others. Practicing these actions helps staff act swiftly and efficiently under pressure.

Communication Exercises: Staying Connected in an Emergency

Clear and effective communication is essential in any emergency. Communication exercises help healthcare staff practice using tools such as radios, intercoms, and alarms. These exercises also teach staff how to convey critical information quickly, such as the location of the threat, the actions being taken, and instructions for staff and patients.

By practicing communication skills, staff can improve their ability to work as a team and respond as one coordinated unit. Communication exercises should emphasize the importance of staying calm, speaking clearly, and following established protocols.

In one of our trainings scenarios, we conducted a patient attempting to escape from the hospital without authorization. In this scenario, a nurse was conducting patient rounds. The nurse walked into a patient's room as the patient removed their hospital gown and put their jeans on. The patient's brother snuck in. As the nurse tried to exit, the brother told the nurse to stop right there and lifted his shirt, showing a gun inside his waistband.

The training taught them to follow all the hostage takers' instructions and every minute or so lift their wrist to look at their watch. This will create curiosity, and when asked by the patient or brother if the nurse has someplace to go, the nurse would reply that this is a hospital, and she is conducting rounds checking on the welfare of patients. If I do not call the nurse's station in a few minutes and tell them I am O.K., they will send security to check on me. When permitted to call, they will say, "Hello, my name is ______, I am in room 123, and everything is A.O.K." and hang up the phone.

When this distress call is made, the person on the other side of the phone will immediately notify security. The elevators will be turned off, directing them to the stairs to leave, where the situation can be dealt with more discreetly and isolated.

If this was not an option and the nurse was forced to exit the room with the patient and as they walked down the hallway, the nurse would act calmly and remove their identification from their uniform and hold it straight down in their hand. This was the first non-verbal distress sign a staff member was in trouble and when other staff noticed this, they would immediately notify security.

If this were not a distress call identified by staff, then before the nurse who was being kidnapped exits the hospital doors, they would drop their identification on the ground, before exiting the hospital. As the situation unfolds, any staff who notices a hospital identification on the floor near an exit should immediately notify security and they would review surveillance footage to gather more information.

These are just a few benefits and ideas for communication exercises.

Feedback Sessions: Learning and Improving

Remember to record your exercises from start to finish, including the debriefing after each drill or exercise. All healthcare staff involved should participate in a debriefing. These debriefing sessions allow staff to discuss what went well, what could have been done better, and identify areas for improvement. Feedback from staff members who participated in the drill and from observers can provide valuable insights into how the emergency response plan can be enhanced.

Debriefing sessions create a continuous learning environment, ensuring that healthcare staff always find ways to improve their readiness for an active assailant event. The sole purpose of debriefing exercises is to “improve future performance” rather than to cast blame.

Building a Culture of Preparedness

Preparedness is not just about conducting exercises but about building a culture where safety is a top priority. Healthcare facilities should encourage staff to be vigilant, to report suspicious activity, and to stay informed about emergency procedures. A culture of preparedness helps create a safe environment where staff are always ready to respond.

Regular training, practice, and open communication all contribute to a culture of preparedness. When everyone understands their role and feels confident in their abilities, the facility becomes safer for patients, visitors, and staff.

Conducting exercises and practicing preparedness is essential for ensuring that healthcare staff are ready to respond to an active assailant event. Staff can build confidence and reinforce their understanding of safety protocols by participating in evacuation and lockdown exercises, communication exercises, and realistic simulations.

Remember, each drill is an opportunity to learn and improve. Through regular practice, feedback, and a commitment to preparedness, healthcare staff can help create a safer environment for everyone.

Chapter 17

Reviewing and Updating Safety Protocols

Safety protocols are a critical part of healthcare facilities. These protocols help keep everyone safe, including patients, staff, and visitors. Over time, buildings, technology, and best practices change, and healthcare facilities must update their safety protocols to stay effective. Regularly reviewing and updating these protocols ensures that the facilities are ready for emergencies and can respond quickly and efficiently to keep everyone safe.

This chapter discusses the importance of regularly reviewing safety protocols, involving staff in these updates, and how the Draft Active Assailant Action Book recommends conducting these reviews. Following these guidelines can help healthcare facilities maintain a strong culture of safety and preparedness.

Why Review and Update Safety Protocols?

Safety protocols are essential because they provide clear instructions for responding to emergencies, from fires to active assailant events. However, protocols are only helpful if they are current and reflect the latest information. In healthcare facilities, where new technology and layouts can change, updating safety protocols ensures everyone knows the best ways to stay safe in an emergency.

For example, evacuation routes or barricade areas may have changed if a facility has undergone renovations. Similarly, new technology, like improved communication systems, can impact how staff members respond in an emergency. Regularly reviewing protocols ensures that staff have the latest and most effective procedures to follow, which can save lives.

Recommended Review Schedule

In addition, a regular review schedule helps keep safety at the forefront of everyone's minds. Staff become more familiar with the protocols, making it easier to remember and follow the guidelines in an emergency.

Involving All Staff in the Review Process

When updating safety protocols, it's essential to involve all staff members. Each staff member brings unique experiences and perspectives that can help identify potential protocol issues. For example, a nurse or an aide who works on a busy floor may notice something others might overlook, like challenges in moving patients quickly when escaping the area.

Involving staff in the review process makes them feel invested in the safety protocols. When staff understand and help shape the protocols, they are more likely to follow them and encourage others to do the same.

This collaboration helps create a culture of safety and teamwork, which is critical in healthcare settings.

Incorporating Lessons Learned from Exercises

Exercises are an excellent way to practice safety protocols and see how they work in real-life scenarios. After each drill, healthcare facilities should hold feedback sessions where staff can discuss what went well and what could be improved. These debriefing sessions can reveal essential lessons that can be used to update the protocols to improve future performance.

For example, if a drill shows that communication between floors is slow, facilities can look at ways to improve communication systems or add more training in this area. By incorporating lessons learned from exercises, facilities can continuously improve their protocols and ensure they are as effective as possible.

Keeping Protocols Up to Date with New Technology

Technology is constantly advancing, and healthcare facilities often adopt new tools that can impact safety protocols. For instance, improved alarm systems, surveillance cameras, or communication devices can make it easier to respond to emergencies. When new technology is introduced, reviewing the protocols and seeing how it can be integrated into safety measures is essential.

For example, if a facility installs a new intercom system, the protocols should include instructions on how to use it to alert staff of an emergency. Keeping up with technological advances helps ensure that safety protocols remain relevant and practical.

Creating a Culture of Continuous Improvement

One of my favorite quotes is," Safety is a shared responsibility." Safety is not a magical book you read, or video you watch or even a pill you take; it requires constant attention and improvement. By regularly reviewing and updating safety protocols, healthcare facilities create a culture of continuous improvement. This culture encourages everyone to stay engaged with safety practices and to be open to changes that can make the facility safer.

Continuous improvement means every protocol update is an opportunity to learn and grow. By fostering this culture, healthcare facilities can maintain high standards of safety and preparedness, which benefits everyone who enters the facility.

There must be a sound system in place for informing and/or training facility staff members whenever there has been an updated or revised protocol.

Remember, safety is everyone's responsibility. By working together and keeping protocols up to date, healthcare facilities can provide a safer environment for everyone.

Chapter 18

Supporting Each Other and Moving Forward After an Emergency

After an active assailant event, everyone involved may feel a range of emotions, from fear and sadness to confusion and uncertainty. In a healthcare setting, staff must support each other and take steps to recover emotionally and mentally. This final chapter focuses on supporting one another and building a path to recovery that helps everyone, including staff and patients, feel safe and secure again.

Recovering from a traumatic event takes time; each person's experience is unique. By creating a strong support network, offering mental health resources, and encouraging open conversations, healthcare teams can help each other heal and move forward. This chapter provides practical and emotional steps for supporting one another after a crisis.

The Importance of Support After a Crisis

Experiencing a traumatic event like an active assailant incident can be deeply distressing. After such an event, it's normal for people to feel uneasy or anxious. Offering support to one another helps to ease these feelings and reminds everyone that they are not alone.

In healthcare settings, staff work closely together and rely on one another in daily routines. After a traumatic event, this sense of teamwork becomes even more critical. By supporting each other, healthcare workers can find strength together, helping everyone feel safer and more confident as they move forward.

Checking in with Colleagues

One simple but powerful way to support each other is to check in on colleagues. A kind word, a listening ear, or a moment to talk can make a big difference. Sometimes, knowing that someone cares can help reduce stress or isolation.

Encouraging open conversations where people feel comfortable expressing their feelings is essential. Not everyone will want to talk right away, and that's okay. Offering a chance to speak when they are ready can make colleagues feel supported and respected. Creating a culture of care and checking in regularly shows that the team values each person's well-being.

Building a Support Network

A support network is a group of people who can provide practical and emotional support. This network can include close colleagues, friends, family members, and mental health professionals. After an active assailant event, it's helpful for healthcare facilities to organize support networks so that everyone knows where to turn for help.

Support networks can also include peer support groups where people with similar experiences can share and listen to each other. Being part of a group that understands what others are going through can be comforting and make it easier to talk about complicated and unsaid feelings.

Providing Mental Health Resources

Mental health resources are a key part of the recovery process. Traumatic events can have a lasting impact on emotional and mental health, and it's essential to provide access to resources like counseling or therapy. Many healthcare facilities have mental health professionals on staff who can offer support.

Providing information about available resources, such as counseling services or hotlines, helps ensure everyone has options for getting help. Encouraging staff to use these resources as needed can make it easier for them to seek help without feeling ashamed or embarrassed.

Here are short references and explanations for some Critical Incident Stress Management (CISM) teams, Peer Support programs, and the "Struggle Well" program in North Carolina:

1. **North Carolina First Responders Peer Support (NCFRPS):** This program is designed to provide confidential peer support services to first responders. It helps deal with the emotional

aftermath of critical incidents by connecting individuals to trained peers who have experienced similar challenges.[63]

2. **NC-LEAP (Law Enforcement Assistance Program):** This program offers peer support services for law enforcement officers, firefighters, and other emergency service personnel. NC-LEAP's services include crisis intervention, emotional support, and guidance from others who understand the unique stressors of first responders.[64]

    - Peer Support for First Responders: This program offers peer-to-peer support to first responders and their families. It emphasizes the importance of talking about mental health struggles with someone who truly understands the pressures of emergency services. [65]

Encouraging Open Conversations

Talking openly about the experience can be a helpful part of the healing process, especially during critical incident debrief. While some people may not feel comfortable sharing their thoughts and feelings right away, creating a safe environment for open conversations allows people to share when they are ready.

Healthcare facilities can host group discussions led by trained professionals to allow staff to talk about their feelings. These sessions should be supportive and judgment-free, helping staff to process their

[63] (NC First Responder Peer Support - North Carolina First Responder Peer Support, 2024)
[64] (Home | NC-LEAP, n.d.)
[65] (FRPSN ORG, 2019)

experiences and hear how others are feeling. Open conversations can also help reduce the stigma around talking about mental health, making it easier for everyone to reach out for support.

Understanding Survivor's Guilt After Surviving an Active Assailant Attack

Surviving a traumatic event like an active assailant attack can lead to many different emotions. One familiar feeling that some people experience is called "survivor's guilt." This is when someone feels guilty for surviving a dangerous situation when others were hurt or didn't make it. Survivors' guilt can be confusing and difficult to handle, especially when combined with the stress of the event itself. Remember, it's okay to feel this way; there are ways to work through it with support and understanding.

What is Survivor's Guilt?

This feeling can come with questions like, "Why did I survive?" or "Could I have done something more to help others?" Even though these thoughts are daily, they can make someone sad, anxious, or ashamed.

Survivor's' guilt is a typical response to traumatic situations and is a type of reaction to the stress and shock of the event. Understanding these feelings are normal can be the first step in managing them.

Why Does Survivor's Guilt Happen?

Survivor's guilt can happen for different reasons. When people survive a traumatic event, they may feel responsible, even if they did nothing wrong. Sometimes, the brain tries to make sense of a scary situation by asking why things happened the way they did.

People might feel they were lucky to survive or didn't deserve to make it when others didn't. These feelings are part of the brain's processing of the trauma, even though they may not make logical sense. Survivor's guilt is a way that the mind tries to cope with the reality of the event.

Common Thoughts and Feelings with Survivor's Guilt

People with survivor's guilt might have different thoughts and feelings. Some common ones include:

1. **Feeling Responsible:** Thinking they could have done something to prevent what happened.
2. **Questioning Why:** Asking, "Why did I survive, and others didn't?"
3. **Sadness and Grief:** Mourning those hurt or lost in the event.
4. **Anxiety:** Feeling worried or fearful that something similar could happen again.

Knowing these feelings are normal responses to a traumatic experience is important. Survivor's guilt is part of the healing process, and understanding these feelings can help in coping with them.

Managing Survivor's Guilt

Managing a survivor's guilt can take time, but there are ways to help ease these feelings. Here are some steps that can help:

1. **Talk About It:** Talking with others about the experience can help release some feelings. Whether it's a friend, family member, or mental health professional, sharing thoughts and feelings can make understanding and accepting them easier.

2. **Remember It's Not Your Fault:** Survivor's guilt often comes with feelings of responsibility, even though the survivor had no control over the situation. It's important to remind oneself that they are not to blame for what happened.

3. **Focus on Self-Care:** Taking care of physical and emotional needs is essential after a traumatic event. This includes getting enough rest, eating well, and relaxing. Self-care helps with recovery and provides the strength to cope with complicated feelings.

4. **Join a Support Group:** Being with others who have gone through similar experiences can be comforting. A support group provides a safe space to share and understand each other's feelings without judgment.

5. **Find Positive Outlets:** Sometimes, doing something positive, like helping others, volunteering, or participating in community activities, can be a way to cope with survivors' guilt. It can provide a sense of purpose and help move forward from the experience.

When to Seek Professional Help

While survivor's guilt is usual, sometimes it can become overwhelming. If feelings of guilt, sadness, or anxiety make it hard to go about daily life, it may be helpful to talk to a mental health professional. Therapists and counselors can provide tools and strategies for managing these feelings.

Seeking help is a positive step toward healing. Remember that survivor's guilt is a part of the trauma recovery process, and getting support can make the journey easier.

Survivor's guilt is a natural response to surviving a traumatic event, such as an active assailant attack. It's normal to feel this way; there are ways to manage these feelings. Talking openly about the experience, practicing self-care, and finding support can help you recover.

Remember, you are not alone, and seeking help is okay. With time, support, and understanding, moving forward and finding peace after a traumatic event is possible.

Rebuilding a Sense of Security

Feeling safe again is a critical part of recovery. After a traumatic event, it's natural for people to feel uncertain or afraid. Rebuilding a sense of security within the healthcare facility helps staff feel more confident and comfortable at work.

Steps to rebuild facility security might include reviewing and updating safety protocols, adding security features like cameras, and ensuring that everyone understands what to do in an emergency.

Knowing that the facility is taking steps to improve safety can help everyone feel more protected and reduce feelings of worry.

Practical Steps for Moving Forward

Moving forward after a traumatic event takes time, but practical steps can make the process easier. These include taking time to rest and recover, setting small goals, and supporting each other.

Some practical steps for recovery include:

1. **Taking Breaks:** Resting yourself is essential after a crisis. Healthcare staff work in high-stress environments, and it's okay to recharge after an emergency.
2. **Setting Goals:** Recovery is a gradual process; setting small goals can make it more manageable. These goals can be personal or work-related, like focusing on completing a task or connecting with a friend.
3. **Celebrating Progress:** Every step forward is an achievement, no matter how small. Recognizing and celebrating progress helps to build confidence and motivation.

These practical steps help healthcare staff care for themselves and move forward one step at a time.

The Role of Leadership in Supporting Recovery

Organizational leaders play a vital role in the recovery process. Leaders can set a positive example and create a supportive environment by showing empathy and understanding. Leaders should encourage open communication, provide access to mental health resources, and show that they care about the well-being of each staff member.

When organizational leaders are actively involved in recovery, it helps staff feel valued and supported. Leadership can also take practical steps, like organizing support sessions, checking in with staff, and ensuring safety measures are reviewed and updated.

Creating a Culture of Healing and Resilience

Building a culture of healing and resilience means creating an environment where everyone feels supported, valued, and safe. In a resilient workplace, people are encouraged to care for themselves and each other, especially after complex events.

To create this culture, healthcare facilities can encourage self-care practices, provide access to wellness programs, and promote the use of support resources. When everyone feels part of a team that cares, facing challenges and recovering from them becomes more manageable.

Resilience is not just about bouncing back but also about learning from experiences and becoming more assertive. Healthcare teams can move forward with renewed strength and confidence by focusing on healing and resilience.

After an active assailant event, supporting each other and moving forward is essential for healing. By checking in on colleagues, building support networks, providing mental health resources, and creating a safe space for open conversations, healthcare teams can help each other recover and regain a sense of security.

Organizational Leaders play an essential role in fostering a culture of resilience and healing, and practical steps like updating safety protocols and encouraging self-care make it easier for everyone to feel safe and supported. Remember, recovery takes time, and asking for help along the way is okay.

Together, healthcare teams can create a supportive, resilient environment where everyone feels valued and ready to move forward, no matter their challenges.

As the author, many ask me about my motivation on this topic. My reply has always been the same. "What answer would you want to hear if your loved one were killed during an active assailant incident? I know mine - what is yours?

References

Legacy Good Samaritan Incident. (2023). Legacy Health. https://www.legacyhealth.org/About/news-and-media/for-the-media/news-releases/2023/Legacy-Good-Samaritan-Incident?utm_source=chatgpt.com

(Legacy Good Samaritan Incident, 2023

Vargas, R. A. (2024, November 13). Oregon hospital sued for $35m by family of security guard shot dead in hallway. The Guardian; The Guardian.https://www.theguardian.com/us-news/2024/nov/13/oregon-hospital-security-guard-death?utm_source=chatgpt.com (Vargas, 2024)

Deliso, M. (2022, June 2). Timeline: How the Tulsa medical office mass shooting unfolded. ABC News. https://abcnews.go.com/US/timeline-tulsa-medical-office-mass-shooting-unfolded/story?id=85138971&utm_source=chatgpt.com (Deliso, 2022)

Simple,. (2025). DocSend - Simple, intelligent, modern content sending. DocSend. https://vistelar.docsend.com/view/2qe69p32n6rmpf8t (Simple, 2025)

News, E. (2018, November 20). Mercy Hospital Shooting: 4 dead, including Chicago Officer Samuel Jimenez and gunman. ABC7 Chicago. https://abc7chicago.com/mercy-hospital-chicago--medical-center-shooting-active-shooter/4720765/?utm_source=chatgpt.com (News, 2018)

News, E. (2018, November 20). Mercy Hospital Shooting: 4 dead, including Chicago Officer Samuel Jimenez and gunman. ABC7 Chicago. https://abc7chicago.com/mercy-hospital-chicago--medical-center-shooting-active-shooter/4720765/?utm_source=chatgpt.com (News, 2018)

Nir, S. M. (2017, June 30). Doctor Opens Fire at Bronx Hospital, Killing a Doctor and Wounding 6. The New York Times. https://www.nytimes.com/2017/06/30/nyregion/bronx-hospital-shooting.html

(Nir, 2017)

Hassan, C., & Martinez, M. (2013, December 17). One person, gunman dead in shooting at Reno medical building. CNN. https://www.cnn.com/2013/12/17/us/reno-hospital-shooting/index.html?utm_source=chatgpt.com (Hassan & Martinez, 2013)

The Repossession of James Edward Pough: Mass Shooting, Baymeadows: Gilmore, Tim: 9781720528647: Amazon.com: Books. (2025). Amazon.com. https://www.amazon.com/Repossession-James-Edward-Pough-Baymeadows/dp/1720528640?utm_source=chatgpt.com (The Repossession of James Edward Pough: Mass Shooting, Baymeadows: Gilmore, Tim: 9781720528647: Amazon.com: Books, 2025)

FBI. (2019). Columbine High School. FBI. https://vault.fbi.gov/Columbine%20High%20School%20 (FBI, 2019)

Peer Support for First Responders: This program offers peer-to-peer support to first responders and their families. It emphasizes the importance of talking about mental health struggles with someone who truly understands the pressures of emergency services.(FRPSN ORG, 2019)

FRPSN ORG. (2019). FRPSN ORG. https://www.frpsn.org/ (FRPSN ORG, 2019)

Home | NC-LEAP. (n.d.). Www.nc-Leap.org. https://www.nc-leap.org/ (Home | NC-LEAP, n.d.)

NC First Responder Peer Support - North Carolina First Responder Peer Support. (2024, June 29). North Carolina First Responder Peer Support. https://ncfrps.org/

(NC First Responder Peer Support - North Carolina First Responder Peer Support, 2024)

Cutting Your Team's Response Time in Half | CriticalArc. (2018, November 27). CriticalArc. https://criticalarc.com/cutting-your-teams-response-time-in-half/?utm_source=chatgpt.com

(Cutting Your Team's Response Time in Half | CriticalArc, 2018)

Mark, M. (2022, June 25). Family of Good Samaritan sues Colorado officer who fatally shot him. Business Insider.

https://www.businessinsider.com/good-samaritan-family-sues-colorado-officer-who-fatally-shot-him-2022-6?utm_source=chatgpt.com (Mark, 2022)

Redirecting. (2025). Google.com. https://www.google.com/url?q=https://www.fbi.gov&sa=D&source=docs&ust=1738590181070163&usg=AOvVaw3vdVPJlMOli5elVBatokmI (Redirecting, 2025)

Disaster Mental Health. (2020). Redcross.org. https://www.redcross.org/about-us/our-work/disaster-relief/disaster-mental-health.html?srsltid=AfmBOoqzAI7bW1xAv_tE1YgMX2ZjWeEj-jZ4IMx_y4sDV0e9Qyb4fai6&utm_source=chatgpt.com (Disaster Mental Health, 2020)

Navigating a Mental Health Crisis. (2024, February 12). NAMI. https://www.nami.org/support-education/publications-reports/guides/navigating-a-mental-health-crisis/?utm_source=chatgpt.com (Navigating a Mental Health Crisis, 2024)

Crisis Counseling Assistance & Training Program. (2025, January 21). Fema.gov. https://www.fema.gov/fact-sheet/crisis-counseling-assistance-training-program?utm_source=chatgpt.com (Crisis Counseling Assistance & Training Program, 2025)

Violence in Healthcare | Blogs | CDC. (2015, March 27). Cdc.gov. https://blogs.cdc.gov/niosh-science-blog/2015/03/27/violence-in-healthcare/?utm_source=chatgpt.com (Violence in Healthcare | Blogs | CDC, 2015)

Workforce Safety and Well-Being: Workplace Violence Prevention Program. (2025). Jointcommission.org. https://www.jointcommission.org/our-priorities/workforce-safety-and-well-being/resource-center/workplace-violence-prevention/workplace-violence-prevention-program/?utm_source=chatgpt.com#t=_StrategiesTab (Workforce Safety and Well-Being: Workplace Violence Prevention Program, 2025)

ICISF. (2024). ICISF. https://icisf.org/?utm_source=chatgpt.com (ICISF, 2024)

Center, N. (2020). VA.gov | Veterans Affairs. Va.gov. https://www.ptsd.va.gov/?utm_source=chatgpt.com (Center, 2020)

Disaster Behavioral Health Resources. (2024). Samhsa.gov. https://www.samhsa.gov/technical-assistance/dtac/resources?utm_source=chatgpt.com (Disaster Behavioral Health Resources, 2024)

National Mass Violence Center | NMVC. (2024). Nmvvrc.org. https://nmvvrc.org/?utm_source=chatgpt.com (National Mass Violence Center | NMVC, 2024)

(2024). Apa.org. https://www.apa.org/ptsd-guideline?utm_source=chatgpt.com (2024)

Young, D. (2018, September 4). Surviving as a Hostage. Police Magazine. https://www.policemag.com/training/article/15346228/surviving-as-a-hostage (Young, 2018)

Walden, M., Lovenstein, A., Ramick, A., Spray, B., Denton, A., McGinley, J., Eisenberg, L., Adams, G., Plunkett, J., Moore, H., Goddard, C., Wooley, C., & McElroy, S. (2021). Perceptions of the Moral Obligations of Pediatric Nurses During an Active Shooter Event in a Children's Hospital. Journal of Pediatric Nursing, 60, 252–259. https://doi.org/10.1016/j.pedn.2021.07.014 (Walden et al., 2021)

Sullivan, M. (2011, June 2). Army major kills 13 people in Fort Hood shooting spree. HISTORY. https://www.history.com/this-day-in-history/army-major-kills-13-people-in-fort-hood-shooting-spree?utm_source=chatgpt.com (Sullivan, 2011)

ACTIVE SHOOTER HOW TO RESPOND. (2008). https://www.dhs.gov/xlibrary/assets/active_shooter_booklet.pdf?utm_source=chatgpt.com (ACTIVE SHOOTER HOW to RESPOND, 2008)

https://www.police1.com/active-shooter/articles/why-move-escape-or-attack-is-superior-to-run-hide-fight-YrpclJaEgKID451c/?utm_source=chatgpt.com (Wood, 2016)

Wood, M. (2016, July 6). Why "Move! Escape or Attack" is superior to "Run, Hide, Fight." Police1. https://www.police1.com/active-shooter/articles/why-move-escape-or-attack-is-superior-to-run-hide-fight-YrpclJaEgKID451c/?utm_source=chatgpt.com (Wood, 2016)

FBI Releases Study on Active Shooter Incidents. (n.d.). Federal Bureau of Investigation. https://www.fbi.gov/news/stories/fbi-releases-study-on-active-shooter-incidents (FBI Releases Study on Active Shooter Incidents, n.d.)

Hospitals, Healthcare Workers Are "Soft Targets" for Shooters. (2024). Relias Media. https://www.reliasmedia.com/articles/hospitals-healthcare-workers-are-soft-targets-for-shooters?utm_source=chatgpt.com (Hospitals, Healthcare Workers Are "Soft Targets" for Shooters, 2024)

Active Attack*. (2025). International Association of Chiefs of Police. https://www.theiacp.org/resources/policy-center-resource/active-attack?utm_source=chatgpt.com (Active Attack*, 2025)

Protective Actions Research. (2025). Fema.gov. https://community.fema.gov/ProtectiveActions/s/article/Active-Shooter-Run-Hide-Fight?utm_source=chatgpt.com (Protective Actions Research, 2025)

FBI Releases Study on Active Shooter Incidents | Federal Bureau of Investigation. (2017). Federal Bureau of Investigation. https://www.fbi.gov/news/stories/fbi-releases-study-on-active-shooter-incidents?utm_source=chatgpt.com (FBI Releases Study on Active Shooter Incidents | Federal Bureau of Investigation, 2017)

Maximino, M. (2015, February 11). Active shooters: U.S. trends and perpetrators' characteristics - The Journalist's Resource. The Journalist's Resource. https://journalistsresource.org/criminal-justice/active-shooters-u-s-mass-killing-trends-perpetrators-characteristics/?utm_source=chatgpt.com (Maximino, 2015)

Nursingworld.org. https://www.nursingworld.org/practice-policy/nursing-excellence/official-position-statements/id/risk-and-responsibility-in-providing-nursing-care/?utm_source=chatgpt.com (2018)

American Nurses Association. (2025). 2025 code of ethics for nurses. Ana.org. https://doi.org/104503749/template_2025NursingCodeOfEthics (American Nurses Association, 2025)

Haddad, L. M., & Geiger, R. A. (2023, August 14). Nursing Ethical Considerations. Nih.gov; StatPearls Publishing. https://www.ncbi.nlm.nih.gov/books/NBK526054/?utm_source=chatgpt.com (Haddad & Geiger, 2023)

Garske, M. (2016, March 24). Anonymous Call Forces 6-Hour Lockdown at Naval Medical Center San Diego. NBC 7 San Diego; NBC San Diego. https://www.nbcsandiego.com/news/local/naval-medical-center-san-diego-orders-staffers-to-shelter-in-place/59876/?utm_source=chatgpt.com (Garske, 2016)

Osha. (2012, February). Healthcare - Workplace Violence | Occupational Safety and Health Administration. Www.osha.gov. https://www.osha.gov/healthcare/workplace-violence (Osha, 2012)

Search Results | CDC. (2023, January 4). Cdc.gov. https://search.cdc.gov/search/?query=active%20shooter&dpage=1 (CDC, 2023)

Osha. (2012, February). Healthcare - Workplace Violence | Occupational Safety and Health Administration. Www.osha.gov. https://www.osha.gov/healthcare/workplace-violence (Osha, 2012)

CDC. (2024, December 4). About Workplace Violence. Violence. https://www.cdc.gov/niosh/violence/about/index.html?utm_source=chatgpt.com (CDC, 2024)

Osha. (2012, February). Healthcare - Workplace Violence | Occupational Safety and Health Administration. Www.osha.gov. https://www.osha.gov/healthcare/workplace-violence (Osha, 2012)

Prevention of Workplace Violence in Healthcare and Social Assistance | Occupational Safety and Health Administration. (n.d.). Www.osha.gov. https://www.osha.gov/laws-regs/federalregister/2016-12-07 (Prevention of Workplace Violence in Healthcare and Social Assistance | Occupational Safety and Health Administration, n.d.)

Healthcare - Workplace Violence | OSHA.gov | Occupational Safety and Health Administration. (2016). Osha.gov. https://www.osha.gov/healthcare/workplace-violence?utm_source=chatgpt.com (Healthcare - Workplace Violence | OSHA.gov | Occupational Safety and Health Administration, 2016)

https://www.google.com/url?q=https://www.dhs.gov/active-shooter-preparedness&sa=D&source=docs&ust=1738251471473039&usg=AOvVaw0cxaeYkbLx_x4lNrttT1mw (Redirecting, 2025)

Dulle, B. (2024, July 15). Man charged after allegedly shooting gun, assaulting staff at St. Luke's. FOX 4 Kansas City WDAF-TV | News, Weather, Sports. https://fox4kc.com/news/man-charged-after-allegedly-shooting-gun-assaulting-staff-at-st-lukes/?utm_source=chatgpt.com (Dulle, 2024)

Rock, A. (2024, May 3). Detroit: Patient Fires Gun at Nurse, Shoots Self at Sinai-Grace Hospital. Campus Safety Magazine. https://www.campussafetymagazine.com/news/detroit-patient-fires-gun-at-nurse-shoots-self-at-sinai-grace-hospital/134668/?utm_source=chatgpt.com (Rock, 2024)

Hammond, E., Vera, A., Pathe, S., Macaya, M., & Trimble, M. (2022, June). June 1, 2022: Multiple people dead in shooting on Tulsa hospital campus. CNN. https://www.cnn.com/us/live-news/tulsa-hospital-shooting-06-01-22/index.html

(Hammond et al., 2022)

News, E. (2018, November 20). Mercy Hospital Shooting: 4 dead, including Chicago Officer Samuel Jimenez and gunman. ABC7 Chicago. https://abc7chicago.com/mercy-hospital-chicago--medical-center-shooting-active-shooter/4720765/?utm_source=chatgpt.com (News, 2018)

Flipsnack. (2024). _Aug 2024 Survey Results Active Assailant End User (1) (2). Flipsnack. https://www.flipsnack.com/C8A5E866AED/_aug-2024-survey-results-active-assailant-end-user-1-2/full-view.html (Flipsnack, 2024)

Dienst, J. (2017, June 30). Doctor Killed, 6 Wounded in NYC Hospital Shooting; Gunman Dead: Police. NBC New York. https://www.nbcnewyork.com/news/local/shooting-bronx-lebanon-hospital-nypd/193061/ (Dienst, 2017)

Payne, E., Conlon, K., & Berlinger, J. (2015, January 21). Boston doctor killed in hospital shooting had treated gunman's mom. CNN. https://www.cnn.com/2015/01/20/justice/boston-hospital-shooting/index.html?utm_source=chatgpt.com (Payne et al., 2015)

Gunman shot dead at St. Vincent's Hospital in Birmingham, Ala. - UPI.com. (2025). Upi.com. https://www.upi.com/Top_News/US/2012/12/15/Police-kill-gunman-at-Alabama-hospital/11281355593379/ (Gunman Shot Dead at St. Vincent's Hospital in Birmingham, Ala. - UPI.com, 2025)

WTVM. (2018, March 28). Memorial held for Doctors Hospital shooting victims 10 years later. Https://Www.wtvm.com; WTVM. https://www.wtvm.com/story/37821958/memorial-held-for-doctors-hospital-shooting-victims-10-years-later/?utm_source=chatgpt.com (WTVM, 2018)

KPLC. (2002, September 5). Shooting death sparks tourism worries in Shreveport. Https://Www.kplctv.com; KPLC. https://www.kplctv.com/story/922535/shooting-death-sparks-tourism-worries-in-shreveport/?utm_source=chatgpt.com (KPLC, 2002)

1991 Royal Oak Post Office shooting: The untold story of a hero who gave his life for others. (2021, November 11). WDIV. https://www.clickondetroit.com/video/news/2021/11/11/1991-royal-oak-post-office-shooting-the-untold-story-of-a-hero-who-gave-his-life-for-others/ (1991 Royal Oak Post Office Shooting: The Untold Story of a Hero Who Gave His Life for Others, 2021)

FBI. (2019). Columbine High School. FBI. https://vault.fbi.gov/Columbine%20High%20School%20 (FBI, 2019)

The Repossession of James Edward Pough: Mass Shooting, Baymeadows: Gilmore, Tim: 9781720528647: Amazon.com: Books. (2025). Amazon.com. https://www.amazon.com/Repossession-James-Edward-Pough-Baymeadows/dp/1720528640?utm_source=chatgpt.com (The Repossession of James Edward Pough: Mass Shooting, Baymeadows: Gilmore, Tim: 9781720528647: Amazon.com: Books, 2025)

Hassan, C., & Martinez, M. (2013, December 17). One person, gunman dead in shooting at Reno medical building. CNN. https://www.cnn.com/2013/12/17/us/reno-hospital-shooting/index.html?utm_source=chatgpt.com (Hassan & Martinez, 2013)

Nir, S. M. (2017, June 30). Doctor Opens Fire at Bronx Hospital, Killing a Doctor and Wounding 6. The New York Times.

https://www.nytimes.com/2017/06/30/nyregion/bronx-hospital-shooting.html (Nir, 2017)

News, E. (2018, November 20). Mercy Hospital Shooting: 4 dead, including Chicago Officer Samuel Jimenez and gunman. ABC7 Chicago. https://abc7chicago.com/mercy-hospital-chicago--medical-center-shooting-active-shooter/4720765/?utm_source=chatgpt.comb (News, 2018)

Deliso, M. (2022, June 2). Timeline: How the Tulsa medical office mass shooting unfolded. ABC News. https://abcnews.go.com/US/timeline-tulsa-medical-office-mass-shooting-unfolded/story?id=85138971&utm_source=chatgpt.com (Deliso, 2022)

Vargas, R. A. (2024, November 13). Oregon hospital sued for $35m by family of security guard shot dead in hallway. The Guardian; The Guardian. https://www.theguardian.com/us-news/2024/nov/13/oregon-hospital-security-guard-death?utm_source=chatgpt.com (Vargas, 2024)

Legacy Good Samaritan Incident. (2023). Legacy Health. https://www.legacyhealth.org/About/news-and-media/for-the-media/news-releases/2023/Legacy-Good-Samaritan-Incident?utm_source=chatgpt.com (Legacy Good Samaritan Incident, 2023)

Blair, J. P., Nichols, T., Burns, D., & Curnutt, J. R. (2013). Active Shooter Events and Response. CRC Press. https://doi.org/10.1201/b14996 (Blair et al., 2013)

Cornell Law School Legal Information Institute. (n.d.). Justifiable Homicide. Retrieved from https://www.law.cornell.edu (Cornell Law School, 2019)

Citation: American Red Cross. (n.d.). What is First Aid? Retrieved from https://www.redcross.org

Lorenzini, S. (2023, November 29). Staying Calm During a Crisis: Managing Yourself in an Emergency - AACN. Www.aacn.org. https://www.aacn.org/blog/staying-calm-during-a-crisis-managing-yourself-in-an-emergency (Lorenzini, 2023)

Osha. (2012, February). Healthcare - Workplace Violence | Occupational Safety and Health Administration. Www.osha.gov. https://www.osha.gov/healthcare/workplace-violence (Osha, 2012)

https://www.google.com/url?q=https://www.fbi.gov&sa=D&source=docs&ust=1738590181070163&usg=AOvVaw3vdVPJlMOli5elVBatokmI (Redirecting, 2025)

U.S. Department of Homeland Security. (2008). Active Shooter: How to Respond. Retrieved from https://www.dhs.gov

Federal Bureau of Investigation. (n.d.). Active Shooter Resources. Retrieved from https://www.fbi.gov

Flipsnack. (2024). _Aug 2024 Survey Results Active Assailant End User (1) (2). Flipsnack. https://www.flipsnack.com/C8A5E866AED/_aug-2024-survey-results-active-assailant-end-user-1-2/full-view.html (Flipstack 2025)

Citation:

Black's Law Dictionary, 11th Edition (2019): Defines an assailant as "a person who attacks another, either physically or verbally."

Legal Example: The term "assailant" is used broadly in both case law and statutory law. For example, in State v. Wiley, 614 So. 2d 862 (La. Ct. App. 1993), Louisiana courts referred to the individual committing the assault as the "assailant."

Active Threat Preparedness | Safety | The George Washington University. (2019). Safety. https://safety.gwu.edu/active-threat-preparedness?utm_source=chatgpt.com (Active Threat Preparedness | Safety | the George Washington University, 2019)

American Red Cross. (2018). American Red Cross. Redcross.org. https://www.redcross.org (American Red Cross, 2018)

U.S. Department of Homeland Security. (2008). Active Shooter: How to Respond. Retrieved from https://www.dhs.gov

Home. (2019). Department of Homeland Security. https://www.dhs.gov (Home, 2019)

FBI. (2016). Welcome to FBI.gov | Federal Bureau of Investigation. Federal Bureau of Investigation. https://www.fbi.gov (FBI, 2016)

Osha. (2012, February). Healthcare - Workplace Violence | Occupational Safety and Health Administration. Www.osha.gov. https://www.osha.gov/healthcare/workplace-violence (Osha, 2012)

Active Threat Preparedness | Safety | The George Washington University. (2019). Safety. https://safety.gwu.edu/active-threat-preparedness?utm_source=chatgpt.com

(Active Threat Preparedness | Safety | the George Washington University, 2019)

Redirecting. (2025). Google.com.

https://www.google.com/url?q=https://www.fbi.gov&sa=D&source=docs&ust=1738590181070163&usg=AOvVaw3vdVPJlMOli5elVBatokmI (Redirecting, 2025)

2019 Virginia Beach shooting - Wikipedia (2025, January 8). 2019 Virginia Beach shooting. Wikipedia; Wikimedia Foundation. (Wikipedia Contributors, 2025)

Washington Navy Yard shooting. (2022, April 2). Wikipedia. https://en.wikipedia.org/wiki/Washington_Navy_Yard_shooting (Washington Navy Yard Shooting, 2022)

Wikipedia Contributors. (2025, January 26). Metropolitan Transportation Authority. Wikipedia; Wikimedia Foundation. (Wikipedia Contributors, 2025)

Made in the USA
Middletown, DE
21 April 2025